Words of Life

From the Father's Heart of Love

Graham J Marriott

Philos Publishing

Published by Philos Publishing

www.philos.org.uk

Words of Life
From the Father's Heart of Love
Copyright © Graham J Marriott
August 2012

A CIP catalogue record of this title
is available from the British Library

Printed by Lightning Source

ISBN 978-0-9572704-0-4

Dedication

This book is dedicated in the first place to the perfect, loving Father I have in God. As I have listened to Him in journaling He has begun to bring healing and wholeness into my life. As I walk with Jesus, through the Spirit, He is still continuing this process. So I dedicate this book and say a big thank you to the Father, the Son and the Holy Spirit.

I also dedicate this book to my wonderful wife Sue. She has also taught me what true love is like and what it is to live it out, day by day. In the early years of our marriage she was often the support I leaned on. But with God's grace we now walk very much together in His love and power. So thank you Sue and may this book be a way of reflecting my heart felt gratitude.

Acknowledgements

My friend Charles Slagle, who has written the preface to this book, has helped me with his advice and also his friendship. Indeed it was hearing him speak and reading his books that inspired me to hear from God for myself. In particular he introduced me to this approach that is referred to as journaling. He has been very kind to read the draft materials and give me feedback.

My daughter, Kerry, who is a trained editor, has been through my draft too. Her 'fine-tooth comb' has edited out all my poor use of the English language. Syntax, grammar, punctuation have all been laid bare to her eagle editorial eye. So a big thank you Kerry. You are a daughter in a million. May this book, as I said to Sue in the dedication, be a way of reflecting my heart felt gratitude to you.

Prefaces

This preface is written by Charles Slagle author of 'From the Father's Heart' and 'An Invitation to Friendship.'[1]

Only crazy people think they 'hear' God! Is that true? Do only insane or eccentric people hear our Heavenly Father? A significant number of (opinionated?) people seem to think so. This includes entire movements and denominations among professing Christians. They assert that God speaks only through the Bible, and to believe otherwise is to undermine the Bible's authority.

But are they right? Is a literal relationship — heart to heart, person to person — with our Creator — the Almighty! — impossible? Or implausible? Would our loving Father (and the Bible actually says "God is Love") show partiality and allow only Adam, Methuselah, Noah, Abraham, Moses, the Old Testament prophets, Jesus, Paul and Christ's earliest apostles to enjoy His literal fellowship and exclude the vast majority of their fellow human beings from that joy?

I don't think so. I really don't. In fact, I know for example that, Graham Marriott, the author of this very book you hold in your hands *hears* God. When I first received his manuscript I called two friends and read them a couple of his letters from God. "Who is this guy?" they both asked. Then they immediately said things such as "That was uncanny; it really spoke into my own situation, my own need".

Then just moments ago, I opened Graham's manuscript and my eyes 'just happened' to fall on the words, "My Child, there is nothing you can do to receive all that I have for you". What? How can this happen? I had just been wondering if I *could do something* to help bring about the answer to a prayer I've been praying ... That tormenting question has lingered in my mind as a lurking shadow for several weeks. Wow! What freedom our Father's words have brought me this evening! Actually, I recognized the voice of our Father (English accent notwithstanding!) because I had already

---

[1] See Bibliography

been hearing it amidst the rumbling rambling of this old, grey matter between my ears! All I needed was Graham Marriott's typed words to 'amplify it to clarity' — so to speak. (Page 4 "The Mighty Niagara")

That, I believe, is Graham's deepest aspiration for publishing some of his prayer-journaling for you to read. He yearns for you to discover that you also hear our Father's voice – all the time. I add my prayer of agreement to Graham's prayer now:

'Gracious Father,

Thank You for allowing Your Eternal Son to visit our world so we could see what You are really like ...and ... what it is like to enjoy a real relationship with You. Jesus said that He did only what He 'saw' You doing and spoke only what He 'heard' You saying. Further, He promised that all who trust in Him will do the same miraculous things that He did, and even greater ones, too!
Dear Father, that still astounds me, even though I have had a personal relationship with You and Jesus and Your Holy Spirit for over four decades! And especially over the last fifteen years!

I pray, along with Graham, that all who read these pages will experience the sheer ecstasy of Your literal Presence and fellowship that we have known. Let the words of this book — many times, for many years — confirm Your Presence and leading to those who read it.

Grant readers courage to take pen and notebook in hand, sit quietly in Your Presence, and trust You to write letters to them, through them, just as You do for and through Graham and myself. Scripture says that You make Your servant-hearted children 'flames of fire'. May the Holy Fire of Your never-failing love enflame them to burn as lights of Your healing hope in our searching, deeply wounded world.

I ask this in the name of our Strong Deliverer, the Son of Your Righteousness, Jesus Christ.

Amen'.

"My Sheep Hear My Voice..." (John 10:27)

Jesus said it! Graham demonstrates it! You can do it!

Many years ago, I read the book *God Calling* by Two Listeners. It was a book of journaling, just like Graham's. I was so amazed that people could hear God's voice and write it down. It seemed like an impossibility to me. What amazing people these "two listeners" must have been. How I hungered to have this experience.

Now, we have the privilege of training others how to hear God's voice. This book, *Words of Life*, is a wonderful demonstration that God is still speaking today. After 500 years of the Church believing there is no living contact between God and man, this wall of separation is being broken down. The Wonderful Counselor is speaking words of healing into our hearts. This book is a demonstration of that fact and His loving words provide healing, inspiration and life!

So enjoy these daily devotionals, and let them call you into doing the same thing that Graham Marriott has done. Learn how to hear His voice, so you can receive His words of life into your own heart on a daily basis. He is no respecter of people. Jesus is speaking to you, just as he has spoken to Graham. Let His fresh daily words spill down over your life, cleansing you, healing you and restoring you.

Graham, thank you for your faithfulness in pursuing a life lived by the Spirit. Thank you for demonstrating in print that God STILL speaks today. Thank you for sharing your innermost heart with us, allowing the blessings you have received to spill over onto us.

Enjoy the words of the Lord.

Mark Virkler - Author of '*4 Keys to Hearing God's Voice*'

Contents

Introduction

God has spoken to us most clearly through His Son Jesus, the Living Word. He has also given us His written word, the Bible. However, He is a living and loving Father God who delights to speak to us his children today. One of the ways of hearing what He is trying to communicate with us is to keep a journal.

> '*Journaling is a way of recording what one senses God is speaking within him. Impressions sensed in the heart are registered in the mind and recorded by the hand. It is similar to the Psalms except that one's journal never becomes Scripture. Rather it is tested by Scripture.*'

This book is taken from my journaling over the years. It is not a substitute for your own walk with God through Jesus His son and the infilling and flow of the Spirit. But many of the things that God has said to me, He would say to you. In the first instance He is always saying as our heavenly Father 'I love you'.

It was reading extracts of Charles Slagle's books[1] that spurred me on to reach out and 'hear' what God was saying to me. So be bold enough in faith through the Spirit, to reach out in your heart, and hear what God is saying to you. And don't forget to write it down, that way you won't forget what He said!

---

[1] 'From the Fathers Heart' and 'An Invitation to Friendship' by Charles Slagle

Chapter 1

Hearing His Voice

Our Heavenly Father (as our perfect parent) longs to have a close, warm and intimate relationship with us, His children. All relationships involve communication. This involves not only speaking to, but listening to the other person, and hearing what they are saying to us.

Sometimes between people who are very close, there are times when no words are necessary. Just the look between two people who are deeply in love can convey so much. The Lord wants to communicate to our hearts and minds at a deep level.

Sometimes it can feel like we are hearing 'through a piece of string'. But at other times the 'inner voice' of His in our hearts seems quite clear to us. As a loving Father he speaks warm and affirming thoughts to us His children.

The following 4 keys[1] as set out by Patti and Mark Virkler may help us in receiving His thoughts:

 Recognize God's voice as spontaneous thoughts which light upon your mind.

 Quiet yourself so you can hear God's voice.

 Look for vision as you pray.

 Write down the flow of thoughts and pictures that come to you.

---

[1] '4 Keys to Hearing God's Voice' by Patti & Mark Virkler

Feeding upon My Word

Isaiah 55:1-2; Ezekiel 3:3; 2 Corinthians 4:7(KJV)

My child,

Listen to My words. Feed upon them, for they will be sweeter than honey to you. Just stand on the fact that you are in Me and I am in you. This is by My wonderful grace and your faith in opening your heart to Me through Jesus My Son. Reach out to Me and I will give you the food you need. This is the bread and milk that my prophet Isaiah spoke of. Continue to open up your heart to Me. Trust Me over all you do which includes your work. Place all your family in My hands and leave them there.

You will learn to hear My voice more closely. But remember all My children are different. The way you receive from Me is completely different to the way others receive. Just be yourself in Me through Jesus. Remember you are a human being and not a human doing. So don't strive. Relax in Me and trust Me in all things. Remember, I see your heart and you are a man after My own heart. Yes, I see your sin, your brokenness and imperfection. But remember My treasure is contained in earthen vessels. I forgive you completely through the blood of Jesus My Son. I am healing the brokenness and helping you to overcome your imperfections. I will continue to flood your life with My grace.

As ever,

Father

Leaving Space

Job 4:16(Amplified); Isaiah 49:1

My child,

Will you listen to My voice? Will you listen to what I say? Will you leave space in which I can speak to you? Remember I love you with an everlasting love, and I assure you I love to hear you speak and to sing My praises. But I also long to reply to you and bring My word to you.

Patiently as ever,

Father

Turmoil

James 4:8

Worrying child,

It is your own turmoil that prevents you from hearing My voice. I am never far from you, believe Me. Let Me deal with your doubts. Give them to Me. For am I not greater than any doubts you may have? Peace, be still. Rest yourself in Me. 'Draw near to Me and I will draw near to you.' I will give you clarity of hearing in due course, just trust Me, and stop fretting about things.

Your ever patient,

Father

The Mighty Niagara

Ephesians 1:8; Ephesians 6:14

My child,

There is nothing in yourself that you
can do to receive all that I have for
you. Remember, how did you receive
your salvation? Did you really do
anything to receive it? The only thing
you did was to come with empty
hands to reach out and receive this
gift of love and life in Jesus My Son.

So why do you think you can do anything to receive the fullness
of my Spirit? All you need to do is to recognise that you are empty
and dry, and then come with a fully open heart. In this attitude I
will pour My Spirit into you. I see your efforts to read my word the
Bible, to pray and to use other spiritual exercises. These are
helpful as channels of my grace. But it is not your effort that
causes my Spirit to flow. It is as I lavish My grace upon you that
you receive the fullness of the Holy Spirit.

Yes, unfortunately you can block it with scepticism, cynicism and
doubts. But when you seek Me and say 'more Lord', what do you
think I will do? What I will do is to open the flood gates of heaven
and send a mighty Niagara of the Spirit upon you.

So relax my child. Stand still and believe. Keep an open heart.
Remember, I love you deeply and unconditionally for you are my
child. And when I look at you I see Jesus' righteousness as a robe
around you and therefore there really is no condemnation! So
freely receive and freely let it flow.

Encouragingly,

Father

Bold Pioneers

Deuteronomy 6:4; Matthew 28:20

My bold pioneers,

What you ask is not difficult for Me, for I can do all things and am in all things (when they are submitted to Me). I know the desires of your hearts and have heard your prayers. Just trust Me and do not question or reason it all out. I will act, but it may not be in the way you expect. Keep listening to My voice and looking to Me, for I am with you always, even when you don't think I am.

Your ever present,

Father

Wait upon Me

1 Kings 19:11-13; Revelation 8:1

My struggling child,

It is good that you reach out to Me and listen to what I say. Yet, like today sometimes I don't say much. Do not worry over this; I am always with you.

Learn to wait upon Me. Be patient for I will speak as and when it is necessary. Learn to trust Me, to have faith, when you need Me, I will speak.

For I will meet your needs according to the riches of My grace. So keep trusting and listening.

Father

The Tortoise

Revelation 2:26; Philippians 3:12-14

My child,

Consider the tortoise. If you remember, the tortoise won the race. He won because he kept going. Some people are like the hare they rush ahead but then give up. But the plodding tortoise gets there in the end, in his own time. Tortoises can move at quite a fair speed when they put their mind to it.

You've been a tortoise in My kingdom. True, you often used to pull yourself into your shell and keep the world at bay. But now you are learning to keep your head and limbs out and make yourself more vulnerable, as you walk in My kingdom. Even the shell has been growing softer and I will continue this process. You'll probably never completely lose your character as a tortoise. But I love tortoises. I can use tortoises. They can play a really effective role in building My kingdom.

I have to keep prodding hares all the time to get them going. So think how much easier I find tortoises. So keep going. Keep your head, arms and feet out; moving for Me. Let Me continue to melt your hardness and in place of it build My warmth and gentleness.

Your transforming,

Father

The Hares

Ezekiel 38:9

My child,

Don't despise the hares. They can and do play a significant part in My kingdom. They can leap ahead and make rapid advances in expanding the kingdom. I need all types in My kingdom working together. So make room in your heart for the hares. I do! So keep working together.

Your loving and caring,

Father

Brain Power

Luke 10:27; 2 Peter 1:13

My wondering child,

It is true that in theory you have an infinite amount of memory. Yes there are billions of neurons in your brain. And if you were like a perfect computer, then your memory capacity would be great with instant recall. But you never had such memory even when you were young. You see you are a human being not a perfect physical computer!

But I love people and can easily live with their limitations. So don't worry about limitations; I don't! I can and do work through people. I actually enjoy it too! So why not enjoy living with Me within your limitations. But these limitations will not stop you achieving My purposes; provided you trust Me and look to Me.

The Mind Designer,

Your maker and Father

Journeying

Written whilst on a train journey

Romans 5:5 (KJV)

My joyful adventurer,

It pleases Me that as you sit beneath the grey skies and the pouring rain, your heart is filled with joy. I know this joy is found in Me and not in the things around you.

See how your heart is filled with love for those around you, even though you do not know them. When your eyes are fixed on Me and My Kingdom, just about everything else falls into place. Great isn't it!

Continue to enjoy Me and My Son. Don't worry about concentrating on Me. My Son's delight was always to point people to Me, His Father and creator of Life. You needn't worry about the Holy Spirit either, for His delight is to focus you on Me and bring My Son closer to you. Please think of us as a team. For together we can achieve My purposes. Apart from us, you will fail; though My Kingdom will always triumph in the end.

Think how easily a train completes a journey when it runs on the right track. So too, when you follow My path will complete your journey successfully. Keep on trying and learning, for I am with you. Enjoy yourself and continue to learn to live adventurously. Give Me joy as you learn to listen to Me and do My will. Don't worry about any minor disasters, I don't!

With love and affection,

Your heavenly Father

Hearing

Psalm 95:8; Song of Songs 5:2; Acts 16:14

My child,

I am with you and will always go with you. My grace is sufficient for you. So just rest back in My grace and do what you have to do. Let Me speak through you to others. Don't worry whether you have made it all up or whether it is all due to your preparation. Trust Me, that I can use you through words you speak.

All I need, is for your heart to stay committed to Me, and that you keep your heart open through the day. It helps if you keep your heart very tender. Do not harden your heart. So enjoy what you do, as I do! Rejoice in what I am doing with you. Continue to look to Me and I will guide you.

Your ever present,

Father

No Holding Back

Psalm 139:13; Ephesians 1:4

My child,

Why do you hold back? Why do you not trust that I am in you and you are in Me? You have always been in Me since you committed your life to Jesus. Even before that I had my hand on you, right through conception and birth. Through your childhood I was beside you.

Why do you doubt, that you can bring My word to others? Do not trust your feelings; but trust Jesus, even if you don't see Him and even if you can't feel Him. He is with you always. Put your hand to those things I give you. I see your desire to reach out, but let Me do it in you and in a way that fits you perfectly.

As ever,

Father

9

Conversing with Jesus

John 14:9; John 20:29

My brother,

I do hear your prayer to know me, Jesus, as a person and not just a name. There are some of My followers who use My name with outward enthusiasm and passion, yet do not know Me very closely. Some of My brothers and sisters even stress the first 'J' in My name with great emphasis. So it is fairly easy for people to use My name and yet not know Me that well.

Although it is true that My name, which represents Me, has great power in itself. Truly My name is a name that is above every name in all of creation.

But as you are aware it was Me that said those who follow me can address God as 'Abba', which means daddy. It is our delight to encourage intimacy. Intimacy implies that we know people in a deeper way than just passing and superficial acquaintances.

So My brother, why not (as someone said recently) use your imagination, guided by My Spirit, to get to know what I am really like as a person? It is true that at the moment I don't have any physical attributes you can look at. But why not picture Me as a man you might talk to, over a cup of coffee in a cafe or over a pint in a pub?

We could talk about anything and everything. You could express any view you like in My presence. Even if your view was outrageous and totally opposed to My kingdom values, I wouldn't recoil from you. You would still experience My full and whole-hearted acceptance. Even if your words rejected Me as a person I would go on accepting you. That's what true unconditional love is like.

However, if you expressed some outrageous view that was very bad and didn't fit with My kingdom of love and light, well what do you think might happen? I would probably with a slightly sad but smiling face start to tell you a story. You might wonder at first why I am sharing this simple and apparently un-related story. But towards the end of the story, because you have My kingdom within you, you might see the point of the story. The false would be exposed and the truth would be made clearer. You call them parables. Some theologians go to great lengths to dissect and disseminate them. I once talked about blind guides straining at gnats and swallowing a camel. Maybe these theologians are missing the gnat of the truth of My kingdom and truly swallowing a heavy indigestible camel!

Sometimes you and I would laugh as we drink. We would laugh at some of the silliness in your society. Imagine that driving a certain car gives you status or even will change your personality instantly! What a hoot! We would even laugh at some of the things My followers, the church, do! And sometimes I would chuckle over you My brother, particularly your silly views of your own worth in My sight. Though you know My laughter, the laughter of heaven, is never cruel. This is unlike some of your contemporary comedians.

True, we might occasionally cry over all the pain and brokenness in the world. But in My company we would not do this too often. For I took all this pain and brokenness and carried it within Myself when I went to the cross. And this pain is felt in the heart of the Father and Myself through the Spirit. So Father and I do not expect our children to have to bear this too much in their hearts. It is too big a burden for the human spirit. Yes, you need to have compassion and care. But don't let this weigh your spirit down.

So maybe this glimpse through your imagination has brought Me a little more into focus as a person. I really am not just a name in your case. You do know Me. Remember I am in you and you are in Me. So rest in Me. Imagine My brotherly arm around you as we walk together through life.

Your brother,

Jesus

11

He is Dancing

This was written during a session of soaking prayer[1]. The music gave me at first a sense of movement amongst the trees. Then later on the music gave me an impression of a picture of waves of gentle surf breaking on a sandy shore

Leviticus 26:4

As I come and dance amongst the trees,
So My Spirit blows and frees.
Lightly I dance all around,
Like rain falling on the ground,
Is My presence to be found.

Like the surf breaking on the shore,
I am always bringing more and more.
The waves keep coming on,
For My power keeps pushing them along.

---

[1] Soaking prayer is a form of meditation. Generally people lay down and quiet music is played. When one is soaking there is no agenda. One just lies quietly 'in His presence'. See www.soakingprayer.net

Hearing My Voice

1 Kings 19:11-13; Ephesians 1:7-8

My dear child,

You keep asking to know Me, and to know Jesus My Son. This fills Me with great delight that your heart is set upon knowing Me. But remember you already know Me, and you also know Jesus My Son. Don't forget that Paul said, 'now we see through a glass dimly'.

But remember there is no meanness on My part for My nature is to lavish My grace upon you. But whilst you are already moving in My Spirit, you still have some weaknesses from your fallen nature. Also if I did reveal Myself fully to you in all My glory, might, majesty and Power, you wouldn't cope with it at the moment. If I let you see Jesus in his ascended and glorified radiance it would overwhelm you. Recall that I only let some of My servants, like Elijah, see a brief glimpse of My glory.

Still through My Son you do know Me and you are learning to hear My voice. I am pleased with you; I take delight in you. Let Me remind you, lovingly, that I accept you fully. So go on, with My voice of love, acceptance and praise in your ears. I also hear your unspoken concern for all your family. I have seen all the difficulties and problems in recent times. Do remember that I love you and My desire is for your well being and that of your family. You will come through this period, but do continue to look to Me.

For now, rest in My acceptance and love. Do not strive to be what you already are in Me. Let this come from within, because I have put it there in Jesus and through My Spirit. Remember you do already know Me well and you are beginning to hear My voice.

As ever, Yours for ever,

Father

Still Your Heart

Psalm 29:11; Psalm 41:12; Psalm 46:10

My child,

I hear your prayers and take delight in you. One thing you need to do, is to learn to still your heart. So many things rush round your mind. Not necessarily bad or evil things, often they are facts and knowledge. But hush your heart in order to listen to Me. Still your mind, in My peace. Rest in My presence. For in this way you will hear Me more clearly and know Me more intimately.

I am always with you, but you need to learn how to recognise this. You need to make some time, maybe just some brief moments during the day, when you can draw close to Me. You can draw close to Me in your inner consciousness, through the steps of stillness and expectancy. I am already close to you, but these steps will help you to recognise our relationship and be able to hear from Me.

Despite your faults and sin, I do take delight in you, because you are a child who seeks Me in your heart, not just in outward actions. So continue to walk with Me, My child, and I will be with you always.

In quietness and peace as always,

Father

Struggling with Sin

Isaiah 8:11; Romans 8:18

My child,

You need to trust more in your ability to hear My voice. Why do you doubt it? Why do you not turn to Me more often and listen to My heart? I know you struggle in the area of holiness and righteousness, but you are not alone in such a struggle. Many of my precious children struggle with sin.

My servant Paul struggled to do the things he should and yet found himself doing those things he shouldn't do. Remember My love is unconditional. I don't turn My back on you when you sin. I love you just the same.

True My love cannot reach those of My children who are deliberately disobedient and turn their backs on Me. But you are not in that category. I do see your desire for holiness and I send My Spirit to help. But you must reach out in faith to believe that through My Spirit I am in you and My strength is with you. Remember I am for you; I am on your side, and I love you with an everlasting love.

Yours as ever,

Father

Listen to My Heart of Love

2 Chronicles 6:13; Isaiah 40:9 (The Message)

My child,

You worry too much about hearing My words. Just still your heart and listen to My heart beating with love for you and all My children. This doesn't really need words. Just picture how a loving parent holds their child close to their chest and puts their arms around them and gives them a big hug. The child's head is close to the parent's heart. No words are needed but love is demonstrated and felt.

Rest in Me, close to My heart of love. Do not worry, the words will come in due course. But for now rest in My love. You are right in that some of your thinking and thoughts do get in the way of hearing My voice. But you are learning these lessons. I see your faithfulness in trusting Me, through all lack of feelings and low periods. I also see how you serve Me and this brings pleasure to Me.

So continue to trust. Relax in My love. Do not worry about the lack of 'words'. Serve Me faithfully. Remember My eternal love is yours for ever and ever.

With my heart beat of love,

Father

His Silent Presence

Jeremiah 31:3; Ephesians 3:21(KJV)

My child,

I see your desire to hear My voice. But sometimes I speak without words. As you sit there in silence, don't you feel My presence deep down in your heart? It doesn't express itself in words. Rather it is that deep assurance that you are Mine and I am yours. My eternal love is always towards you. You know My word, 'I have loved you with an everlasting love.' Just rest in this assurance of My never ending love. Don't worry about hearing specific words. But do not fret yourself, I will speak to you clearly in due course. For now just trust Me. Not that you really have any choice. But rest in Me. Relax and know My love that is towards you and all My children at all times and in all places. Do move forward in your exploration of Me. Don't worry if you can't take it all in at first. Picture the smile on My face as I see you continually reaching out to Me, even in a wilderness. But you are not really in a wilderness, you are in the foothills of the knowledge of Me. Keep climbing. Keep rejoicing; continue to praise Me and exalt Jesus, for we are with you for ever and ever, world without end.

Father

Draw Near to Me

Isaiah 43:19; James 4:8

My child,

You so often wait for Me to speak, and you think you have heard nothing. Yet My word is within you, not out there. 'Draw near to Me and I will draw near to you.'

Continue to do those things which I have put before you. But don't think things will continue as they have before. I will do a new thing. But don't wait for it to come, or try to bring it about. Just continue to serve Me. And as you serve Me, this new thing will come upon you, as I pour it upon you.

As I have already said before to you, do not worry if you don't seem to hear My voice. Just trust that I am in you and you are in Me. I will bless you. Just continue to serve Me, but do it with a smile upon your face and joy in your heart. For I love you as My precious child, even if you think you are a bit different.

For I remain as ever and forever,

Your Father

Age Doesn't Count!

Psalm 92:14; Isaiah 46:4; Ephesians 1:8;

My son,

It may have seemed as if I haven't been speaking lately. But you have been crying out to Me so much that you haven't had the space to listen. But My heart delights to see how you have this desire for more of Me. I see your prayer to let the fire fall. Yet, I also see your apprehension. You wonder whether you really desire the fire because of what it might cost. But I also see the desire in your heart to move forward in the Kingdom. I see your desire not to stand still. I have felt your frustration of not moving forward in these recent days. I also see your desire to serve Me through your preaching and praying for others. Yes, I also see you feel inadequate. I know you long to see My Spirit move and for people to be transformed. But oh if you could only see the joy in My heart and the smile on My face as I see your desire for spiritual growth and your willingness to serve Me.

Despite your age I will use you. You can be a father to My children. My Kingdom needs those mature in years, and people who despite their age are not going to just settle down and just occupy a pew! I will lead you forward. I will open up opportunities for you. Don't look at your inadequacy, look to Me the source of life. See again with fresh eyes all that Jesus has made possible for you. Remember what you often mention when preaching that 'I have lavished My grace upon you'. I have given you My Spirit. Let him lead you. Let Him guide you. Learn to trust Me in all things. Feed on My written word but let My Spirit enliven it. Yes, often much of your character comes through, but do not despise this. For I can use people's different characteristics if they are looking to Me, serving Me and open to My Spirit. So do relax, My son, I am truly pleased with you, for My grace does indeed rest upon you.

Lovingly,

Father

What is Faith Like?

Proverbs 2:2; Matthew 17:20

My child,

What do you imagine faith is like? Do you feel you should have absolute clarity and certainty? No, faith is trusting in Me and My word. It is stepping out even though all is not clear and set in 'cast iron'. Remember it can be like the smallest of seeds and yet when planted can grow to be a mighty tree.

What do you imagine My voice is like? Do you expect to hear Me speaking in almost audible words? Haven't My prophets always looked to hear the still small voice within? It is indeed a mixture of imagination, inspiration, perspiration and intuition as someone once said.

But you need to first fix your eyes on Jesus My Son. Then quiet your heart child. Put away all distractions. Finally open the ears of your heart to hear My words within the imagination of your mind. Also open the eyes of your heart to see the pictures I can drop in your mind.

Will you make mistakes? Of course! But I would rather you make the odd mistake here and there, than have the dry arid desert of a life that is never reaching out in faith to hear My word and see My visions. One of the keys, as you have done, is to set your heart on knowing and serving Me. Another key is to continually invite My Spirit to come into your life. Continue to cry, 'more Lord' and 'Come Holy Spirit, come'.

But relax. For if you become tense you will find it so much harder to hear My thoughts. Do, if necessary learn to laugh with heavenly joy and delight. For you will find a lightness in *your* spirit will make the entrance of My Spirit so much easier to flow. You will never have absolute certainty, but you will always have Me. I will grow your faith but let Me plant it within you and water it with My mighty Spirit.

Remember, I will say it again; I take great delight in you child, for you are a man after My own heart. Don't dwell on your flaws and weaknesses, but rejoice first and foremost, that I am in you and you are in Me, through Jesus My Son. Then rejoice in all that I have done in your life so far and all that I am going to do in the future. So relax, enjoy and delight in Me.

With big hugs,

Abba Father

Clamours in Your Mind

1 Kings 19:11-12; Psalm 23:2

My child,

It is in your heart and through your heart that you hear My voice. There are so many things clamouring in your mind that you find it difficult to hear My still small voice. I do appreciate how your mind is assaulted with so many ideas and thoughts. For your society overloads your senses with images and sounds all the time.

But let Me lead you by the still waters and in that place you will hear My gentle voice. Walk hand in hand with Jesus My Son, through the Spirit. For He will lead you to Me, your heavenly Father with My large and loving heart of love. This heart is wide open to you. Peace, be still My child.

In the gentleness of My love,

Father

My Intimate Presence

Proverbs 5:15

My child,

I see your thirsting heart that longs to know My intimate presence. The key to finding this is seek Me with all your heart. For then you will enter My intimate presence. Your awareness of me, will be very real inside of you. But I see your present disappointment that you are not experiencing this to any great depth, at the moment. And I know you understand that you cannot achieve this by effort or striving.

However, let Me give you an illustration or picture, My child. My intimate presence is like the water at the bottom of a deep well. True you occasionally gain a glimpse of it as you hear the water gurgling around from deep down in the depths. But you need to lower the bucket down to the water. And ask yourself the question, does it take any effort to lower the bucket? No! Gravity does the work of lowering the bucket. My heart is longing to have deep intimacy with all My  children. So I will always pull the bucket deeper, drawing My children into the deep water of intimacy with Me. All you need to do is to lower the bucket. You need to make time and space, like all My children, to develop this intimacy.

As the bucket goes lower and lower you will start to hear the gurgling of the water more clearly. So as you go deeper, you will begin to hear My heart more and more closely. (But do remember it is not by your effort that I am drawing you into this intimacy.)

But then eventually the bucket reaches, and is immersed in, the water at the bottom of the well. Then in the same way you will know Me fully, you will know My intimate presence. As you have been led to believe, every part of you will be filled with My presence.

Remember My child that this is only a picture. But maybe it will encourage you to seek Me with all your heart. And it will keep you from striving. It really is not by power or by might. It is My Spirit that is drawing you deeper, as you effectively lower the bucket in terms of seeking My intimate presence.

Oh how I long to share a deep, face to face intimacy with you on a regular basis.

But as always I love you fully and completely forever,

Father

Cultivate Quiet Moments

Psalm 46:10; Zephaniah 3:17

My child,

In silence and solitude, you need to dwell in the secret place. A place no one else shares with you, except Me. And I often dwell there in silence. No words do I speak. But My love fills the atmosphere, like a sweet perfume. And if you rest in this secret place, you will sense My presence.

You see, you human beings have lost your natural spirituality. So many, even some of My children, rush here and there, with such busy and noisy lives. How on earth, or even 'by heaven', do they think they will connect to Me? After all I have said clearly, 'Be still and know that I am God'.

So My child learn to rest in Me. You do not need to strive or make any huge efforts. I am with you, always. Sometimes, when you are busy, you may not sense that I am there. That's Ok. Because I am with you every moment of every day, and in each step of the way.

But cultivate quiet and peaceful moments. There you can rest in Me and I in you. In this place you will be very aware of your sense of being, for that has been given by Me. And you will learn to recognise, yes and even feel, My presence. Practising 'the presence of God', is not that difficult. Remember the example of a simple monk, washing dishes in the kitchen of a monastery who learnt to know My presence constantly.

Oh, how I love you My child, if you could only see fully into My heart or in your case know what I feel towards you. If I chuckle about this, or over you, it is with the laughter of a loving and delighted father.

But I am transforming you and you are growing closer in your relationship to Me. So shalom, peace My child, and press on with My songs of love and deliverance ringing in your ears.

Your ever present,

Father

Shutting Out the Cacophony

Psalm 36:9; 2 Corinthians 5:7 (KJV)

My child,

Do you not begin to feel My Spirit rising up within you? However, remember, you walk by faith, not by sight, nor even by your feelings. Faith is placing your trust in Me, despite what you feel or think. Even when you feel in a 'wilderness' or a 'hard' place, continue to trust that I am with you. That's what faith is all about.

Do realise you walk with Me and My Son Jesus on the pathway of life? You indeed have put your feet on 'the way'. Continue to walk along this pathway of life. Continue to feed upon My Word, the Bible, but don't make it a burden or a duty. Rather make it a joy, as you feed upon Me through reading its words.

Do continue to pray. But please be natural. Oh, how religious prayers bore Me! Remember too, that prayer is a conversation with Me. It is a two way thing. You speak to Me and I speak to you. But to hear My voice you will have to quieten your spirit. You need to shut out the 'cacophony' of the 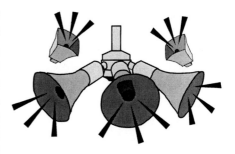 world. You need to discard the lies, whispered to you by the enemy. Remember Jesus is Himself your peace. Resting in that peace you will hear My voice. It will not very often be long words of instruction or teaching. Rather most of the time it will be words of love. I seek to encourage you, just as I seek to encourage all my children, with constant words of love.

Remember, I am love and Jesus was the greatest expression of My love in dying for you, and all My children, on the cross. So sit in peace. Drink from My fountain of life, the eternal words of love.

Clearly as always,

Abba Father

The Storehouse of My Word

Psalm 119:105; Ezekiel 3:3

My adventurous child,

The picture I have given you is that of the entrance to the storehouse of My word. It is a veritable treasure of delights. On the shelves are all the many delightful aspects and subjects you can examine.

You could just stand outside it and look. Some of My children are like that. They never open or enter My Word. Let alone actually devour it.

You could go just inside and examine the things closest at hand. But My invitation is to go wherever you like in this storehouse. Take down anything that catches your fancy. Take it down and examine it to your heart's content. I know in your case I hardly need to say this. But the invitation is to you and all My children. Explore all of My Word. Go where you like. Examine it for all your worth.

And remember I told some of My prophets to eat My Word or scroll. When they did this they found it was sweet as honey to them. So I encourage you feed upon My Word. Take it down, examine it thoroughly and absorb it full into yourself.

And then through My Spirit you can live it out. So go ahead My adventurous one, explore the full treasure house of My Word.

Invitingly,

Father

Chapter 2

Seeing Through the Natural

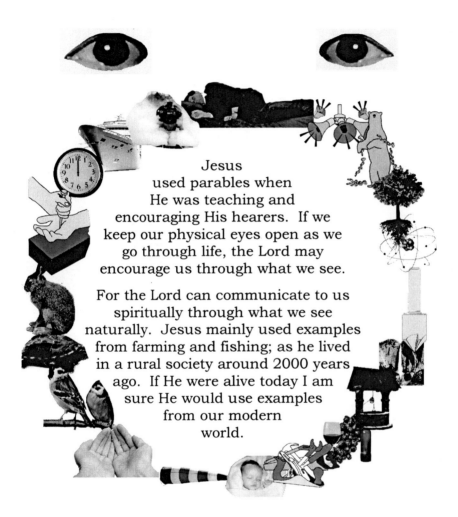

Jesus used parables when He was teaching and encouraging His hearers. If we keep our physical eyes open as we go through life, the Lord may encourage us through what we see.

For the Lord can communicate to us spiritually through what we see naturally. Jesus mainly used examples from farming and fishing; as he lived in a rural society around 2000 years ago. If He were alive today I am sure He would use examples from our modern world.

Many of the examples in this chapter come from the world around us today.

May the Lord encourage and uplift you as you read them and help you to learn to see the Spiritual through the natural.

God's Waterfall of Love

Psalm 104:10; Song of Songs 4:15

My child,

My love is like a waterfall; a mighty Niagara of forgiveness and grace. Stand under My waterfall. Let it flow over you. Let it saturate you with My love and My power. Let it fill you up so full that you overflow, becoming a miniature waterfall. So that you are a reflection of My nature of love and grace. The mighty waterfalls in nature start their journeys high up in the mountains. My waterfall of love starts in My heart of love. It flows through the cross, gathers power in the resurrection and finally floods out through the day of Pentecost and beyond. It is a continual flow of My love and My grace. Flowing down through the years of time and for all eternity. Let it flow; let it grow; for all eternity.

Flowing in love forever,

Father

The River of His Love

Psalm 1:3; Ezekiel 47:12

My child,

Like a river flows My love. This river is truly the flow of My Spirit. Remember the Psalmist says that those who truly follow Me in their hearts are like a tree planted by a river. Their roots go deep down and draw up My life-giving Spirit. And My Spirit brings the love, the wholeness and healing that they need. In turn they can let this flow  to others. For so will My children yield fruit in due course. How could they not do so, when My Spirit of life is flowing through them?

So don't struggle My child, for you are one of those trees planted by My stream of life and love. Just let your roots draw up My Spirit like sap into your very being. For He will bring the love you need. He will also bring healing, wholeness and freedom. So quietly rest by My river of eternal and unchanging love.

Flowing with you,

Father

An Open Door

Revelation 3:7

My child,

See I set before you an open door and no man can close it. This is My doorway of opportunity and blessing. Just continue to look to Me and trust My love and protection. I am your defence; your strong protector, your shield and sword. Rest in Me now and for ever more. For I am yours for ever and ever.

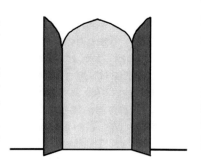

Encouragingly,

Father

Gripping the Rock

1 Samuel 2:2; Psalm 18:2; Ephesians 6:15-17

My champion,

See, My child, I continually set your feet on the rock of Jesus and I provide you with the good news boots to grip this rock.

Stand still and see the victory I will bring about in your life as you wield the sword of My Spirit.

I rejoice over you with My songs of deliverance.
I rejoice in the progress you are making as you open up to Me. My child you are learning the lessons really well. You are rising up in My Power. But remember it comes from Me, not from yourself. I will use you but let Me show you the way.

Constantly,

Father

As Certain as the Sunrise

Judges 5:31; 2 Samuel 23:4

My child,

As certain as the sunrise, is My love for you. It will come afresh to you each day. Light will break into your life. I know your thoughts before you even think them. I see your yearning for more of Me. I hear the cry of your heart, when it is expressed without words. Your desire to know Me more thrills Me to the centre of My being. This desire to be fully open to My Spirit brings pleasure to My heart. But remember don't be too hard on yourself.

Believe Me My child you are in a good place, if you look back you will see the place where you have come from. Then in the light of this consider where you are in Me. Gone is your depression. You are achieving so much in Me. I see all the things you are doing to help build My Kingdom, particularly all your prayers for people. There is joy in your heart, though I know you would like more. There is a lightness in your spirit, but even this I know you would like to grow.

I know you really want to sense My presence in you and to hear My voice more clearly, particularly for others. But this is growing and will come. Take it from Me, how delighted I am with you and in you. Don't strive quite so much, just continue to walk by faith in Me. For I am at work in you to help build My kingdom and at the same time to bring pleasure to you.

Constantly yours,

Father

Climb like a Rocket

Isaiah 60:1; Philippians 2:15

My child,

First you light the blue touch paper
and not very much seems to happen.
There is just a small red glow. Then
a bright light comes from the rear and
up shoots the rocket into the sky.
Going faster; climbing higher; then in
the heavens it burst forth into its
glorious display.

So too will your life be. At the moment
it's just the small glow pregnant with potential. But soon you will
climb up. Then My glory will shine through you to others.
Remember it's My power that will cause you to rise. It's My glory
that you display in your life. So be patient with the small red glow
at the moment.

Your heavenly,

'Firework Master'

God's Countersinking

John 15:6; Ephesians 2:10

My work in progress,

I am countersinking your life so that you will be able to fit
more easily into My kingdom. It is not a destruction of
the real you, but rather a close partnership of Me fitting
into your life.

The countersinking does cut away some of the rough
material of sinful patterns, but in its place is left the
smooth and cleansed place. So that Jesus can fit right into
your life in the perfect relationship that it is meant to be.
Let Me do my work in you. For I really do love you with
an everlasting love, My child.

Father

Sailing before the Wind

2 Peter 1:20-21

My dear child,

You are like a fine old sailing ship with three masts. But your sails are all furled. The ship is sound and the wind is all around you, but it is not filling the sails and driving the ship along. This is because the sails are not raised! You need to learn how to unfurl and raise your sails, so you receive the power from the wind of the Holy Spirit. For He is all around you. Never fear that you can't do this. All things are possible with Me, only believe. I will help you as you keep looking  to Me. I will reveal what you need in due course. Do be patient. But also be expectant, for I will continue to meet your needs in the future.

Your never-changing,

Father

True Type Fonts

Matthew 5:16; Galatians 5:22-23

My children,

On computers there are 'True Type' (TT) fonts. These fonts have the same appearance on the computer screen as they do on the printed page. Other non-TT fonts appear to change their appearance. That is they look different on the computer screen to how look on the printed page.

Some of My children regrettably are like that. They change their appearance outside of a church meeting. Inside church they are kind and lovely. However, at home or work they do not exhibit such love and holiness.

I want My children to be like 'True Type' fonts. That is My children should always appear the same where ever they go. Their lives should reflect the character of Jesus, exhibiting the Fruit of the Spirit, in all places and circumstances. So let modern technology teach you some of My unchanging lessons of the Kingdom.

Yours truly unchanging for ever,

Father

My Gentle Rain

Psalm 72:6

My child,

Hear the sound of My voice. It is like the sound of gentle rain falling on to the dry earth. With it comes an aroma of freshness and new life. Reach out to hear My voice; My voice of life. For I have the words of life. You have found them, but continue to reach out for more of them.

Refreshingly as ever,

Father

The Warmth of My Love

Judges 5:31; Psalm 84:11

My child

As you sit there in the sun, let the warmth of My love permeate your very being. For My love is endless. My love is freely given. So freely receive it in your heart. Let it drive away any misbelief from your heart and mind.

Remember you are mine and I am yours through Jesus My Son, forever. On the cross He demonstrated My magnanimous love. He reconciled you to Me, so that we are now closer than a brother or sister. Let My love flood your heart and drive away any doubts or fears.

For I remain yours forever and ever,

Eternal Father

Relax!

Written on a train when journey was delayed

Matthew 6:28; Luke 12:26

My child

Why worry, especially about that which you cannot change. You might as well throw water against a rock! Only My mighty power can change the unmoveable. Even then it is not always accomplished in a short period, but may take years to bring about; in just the same way as the wind and rain slowly change the hard and unmoveable stone. I am glad you are learning to sit back and relax when the things around you are frustrating.

Even though the train is delayed and it seemed hopeless in getting there on time, you kept going. I like that; it brings pleasure to me. Steadfastness is an attribute of character that I delight in. Didn't My son exhibit it as He moved towards his death on the cross. So keep looking to me and trusting in My grace. I will continue to heal and restore you. You will continually experience My salvation in your life. Don't worry about the things around you, but set your sight on me and My son.

Your unchanging and unmoveable,

Father

No Going Back

Judges 7:19-20

My child,

Remember how Gideon's men, who were few in number, broke their earthenware jars. This meant that there was 'no going back'. Now their lights were fully revealed. The enemy would now know exactly where they were. But much more, in the breaking of the jars, was My power and My glory revealed.

So child, don't go back. Go forward. Remember, numbers don't matter. Strength doesn't matter. Break the jar, and release My power into any situation.

Your all powerful and loving,

Father

His Tools are to Hand

Genesis 4:22; 1 Thessalonians 5:11

My child

The tools you need are right at your feet. As you pick up the tools you will find they fit your hands perfectly. I hear your cry to know My Son Jesus better. And I do hear your cries of repentance. They reach My throne. Do learn to rest in Me. Do not strive. I will bring these things into your life. But just

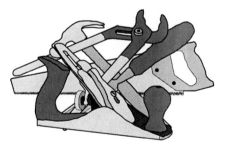

relax in the knowledge, that you are in Me, through your faith in Jesus. And this is all by My grace. Remember you do not have to work for My blessings. All you have to do is to be open. Go through life, trusting you are in Me and that I through My Spirit am in you. Do remember to encourage and up-build My people.

Yours working with you,

Father

Take Off

Written at an airport whilst waiting for a flight.

Isaiah 40:31

My child,

See how easily the aircraft lifts off the runway as the pilot eases gently back on the 'stick'. Such a small change in the angle of the wings lifts the aircraft up into the sky. (Like the eagle it begins to soar.) But all this comes from the immense power of the engines that are thrusting it down the runway.

So too if you want to rise up and soar you must allow the power of My Spirit to flow. Although the power of My Spirit is usually silent and quiet, though not always! It requires no major effort on your part to soar as on eagles' wings. All you need is to gently apply the pressure and to start to lift your wings. Then I will cause you to soar and rise up. So start to move forward like the plane down the runway and I can do the rest.

With gentle power,

Father

A Bend in the River

Isaiah 57:6(KJV); Isaiah 66:12

My child,

Sometimes a river comes to a sharp bend. The flow of the river almost seems to stop. It is as if the river has lost its sense of direction. Also the bank often starts to be eroded at that point.

Your life is at one of these bends in the river. It may appear that you have lost your sense of direction. But think of it as a transition and more of a change of direction. Also at this point, some things are being taken away. The poor things from your childhood are being eroded away.

But remember, does the river stop flowing at the bend? True it may slow up, but it is still flowing. So too I am still flowing in your life. It may be harder to see or feel this at the moment. But trust Me, I am in you and you are in Me. We are flowing together. It may be more slowly and around a difficult bend or corner. But you will come into a straighter section in due course, where we flow more easily together.

So rest easy and in tranquillity. Remember often at these bends, are trees, almost dipping their branches in the water. It is often a place of peace, quiet and rest. So be at peace My child, despite some of the uncertainty. Remember Jesus, My Son, is your peace.

Restfully,

Father

Our Roots in Him

Job 8:16; Job 18:6

My child,

See how the flowers you have before you, have opened up, in response to the light. Also they are drawing up the water through their stems.

So too, your life will open up to the light of Jesus My Son. You have put your roots down deep into My Son Jesus, as the flowers have in the water. Draw upon Him for your strength. Trust your position in Me, through Jesus. Let Me fill you a fresh with My Spirit. Accept that this is happening even when you don't feel it. Go to places where you can be in the presence of Jesus My Son, so He can open you up. But do relax; do trust; and do enjoy My presence, for I enjoy yours.

With my love shining upon you,

Father

The Perfumed Candle

Matthew 5:16; John 9:5; 2 Corinthians 2:15

My children,

My love is like a perfumed candle. In the midst of the darkness, it provides light. Not however the harsh man-made light you are so used to. Rather it is the warm and gentle light of love that softens the harshness and coldness around it. There is also warmth about this light. As it burns it omits a sweet fragrance. A sweetness that fills the air. So it is, with My Love. Whilst I am the source of light and love, you are also meant to be centres of light to people in the darkness around you. Remember Jesus said you weren't to hide your lights under an old bucket.

So too, you mustn't hide your light under 'churchianity' or 'religiosity'. Rather take the light of My love to those around you. However, it is good that as a church you combine your lights together. So you can mutually encourage one another. Remember Jesus said, 'I am the light of the world'. He also said, 'Let your lights so shine, that people will glorify God'. So let your lights burn in the darkness, spreading the light and perfume of My Love, to those around you.

Enlighteningly,

Father

A Toothless Enemy

Ephesians 6:16; James 4:7

My child,

You already have My strength within you. But continue to listen to My voice. Rejoice in the freedom I give you in Jesus My Son. Continue to walk forward in Kingdom power. I know you so often don't believe it is there in you. But trust Me child, My power is in you through My Spirit. All you need to do is to walk forward trusting that you are in Me and I am in you.

Why do you believe the lies and half-truths the enemy flings at you? Wield the shield of faith. Sometimes you let your own doubts and misbeliefs rob you of the joy of walking with Me by faith. But, O how I love you. I see into your heart that longs to serve Me. I see your desire to worship Me. I see your longing to continually enter My throne room. Come in My child the way is always open through the blood that Jesus shed for you.

Learn to laugh more both at yourself and the foolishness of others. Particularly laugh at the toothless lion of your enemy. In Christ he really has no power over you. But he does love to snarl and snap at times. Resist him in the name of Jesus. Remember, greater is He that is in you than he that is in the world. I will lead you, just trust Me My child. Remember My timing is perfect but might not meet your timescales. But for now relax in My peace; trust in My Son and open your life to My Spirit.

Your faithful and constantly patient,

Father

A Time of Preparation

Ecclesiastes 3:1-8

My child,

Do be patient, even though it is not in your nature. Look at the rocks around you. Were they formed and shaped in five minutes? No! Rather, the action of all the elements shaped them. So too I do not always bring things to pass instantly in My children's lives.

But don't worry! I am not saying the wait will be that long. The period you are in now is a time I often place My children in. It is a time of preparation. Would you really be ready for what I might reveal? I see your willing heart, but I also know your evaluating and analytical mind! So treat this as a time of preparation for what is to come. A time to learn, a time to change and a time to start to move forward in a new way.

Your ever caring ever sharing,

Father

The Wind of the Spirit

Psalm 95:8; Ephesians 5:18-19; Hebrews 3:6-8

My children,

Hear how powerfully the wind is blowing. You do not see it. Yet you hear it and can see its effect. So it is with the Holy Spirit. You cannot see Him. Yet you can hear Him and see His effect in people's lives.

The wind doesn't always blow so powerfully. Sometimes it is but a gentle refreshing breeze. So too sometimes My Spirit moves powerfully, particularly in breaking the enemy's strongholds. But usually in My children it is the gentle refreshing life-giving breeze of the Spirit that they experience. Because He is so gentle it is easy to resist Him. Only a small amount of unbelief, stubbornness or disobedience will completely block the movement of My Spirit in people's hearts. Therefore keep your hearts open to Me. Do not harden your hearts as the children of Israel did in the wilderness. Instead, let My love, the love expressed in and through Jesus, keep your hearts open and soft to My Word.

Refreshingly,

Father

New Wine

2 Kings 18:32; Psalm 104:15

My child,

I am the Vine, you are a branch, and I desire you to bear much fruit. It is as My life flows through you that you produce the fruit. And the fruit of the vine is grapes. And from the grapes comes wine.

But think of the wine-making process near the beginning. It doesn't look very nice when it's bubbling away in the fermentation process. But eventually it will be crystal clear and very good to drink.

So too, your life is in effect 'fermenting' and My life is at work within you. So also, will your life in due course flow with the clear wine of life. Just trust Me, that I am at work in you. It may seem messy and even smelly, as it is during the wine-making process, but I am doing this work in your life. This process is not a sign of My judgement, but rather a sign of My Love. It is a manifestation of My goodness, towards you. If I didn't love you I wouldn't be letting this happen. It is part of a preparation process. So take heart My child, for I do this work with much gladness.

With transforming love,

Father

Love beyond Human Sight

Psalm 36:5; Psalm 103:17

My child,

As far as you can see I will always love you. When you travel forward towards this horizon it keeps moving forward in front of you. So my love for you keeps moving forward with you. Even if you could go over the horizon beyond human sight, I would still love you. I truly love you through all ages. Why oh why would you doubt it? I know you don't often feel it, but trust Me when I say wherever  you go, whatever you can see and as far as you can see, I love you.

I see you in all the things you do at, 'work, rest or play'! There I am beside you watching over your shoulder. I like the way you stick at problems and your unwillingness to give up until the task is finished. Can you not see how much I like you, for some of your characteristics are like mine? Call it faithfulness; for I never give up on My desire to save the world. Sometimes I see your frustration when you just can't hack things. It mirrors some of My frustration when I just can't get people, even you, to see I love them and even like them. So this is just one aspect that I like about you and know it reflects part of My character. So let's walk together through life.

With you wherever you go,

Father

Passion for Jesus

2 Timothy 1:6

My children,

At the heart of a steam locomotive is a very hot fire. This is fanned by a very strong draft of air to produce the high temperatures. It is these high temperatures that generate all the steam that produces the power to drive the locomotive forward.

At the heart of your lives there needs to be a passion for Jesus. This fire needs to be fanned by the wind of My Spirit. It will be this that will produce the power in your lives that will drive you forward in building My kingdom; both in your lives and the lives of others.

Motivating you,

Father

Communicating Gently

1 Kings 19:11-12

My child,

As you see the waves breaking over the beach, I'm sure you are aware of the mighty forces that produce the tides and the waves. Yet here the waves are breaking fairly gently on the sand. So too My power is awesome and mighty. Yet I am a gentle creator God who most of the time holds back such power so that it doesn't overwhelm people. My power is also a redeeming power that has at its heart healing and salvation. Such power is indeed available to you through My mighty dynamic Spirit. He is the one that allows such power to come upon you and move through you. Such power flowing through you can touch other people's lives with healing and wholeness. He is also the power that will prevent you from falling completely and will restore you if you do stumble.

As you hear the sound of the waves breaking on the beach, the ripple of the water as it runs over the sand let it remind you that I speak to people. Much of My communication and speech is not with words but in the quietness like the sound on this beach where the waves are gently breaking on the sand and there are birds' songs in the air. I can thunder and roar when I need to. But to My children I speak in gentleness and tenderness; in a still small quiet voice. So often in the midst of the world's clamour they miss it. So remember My child, still your heart and mind and you will hear Me speaking. Speaking eternal words of love and life.

Tenderly and quietly,

Father

The Stream of the Kingdom

Psalm 46:4; Proverbs 18:14; Isaiah 33:21; Isaiah 43:19

My child,

My Kingdom is like a never ending stream. The key thing is for you to be in this stream.

In some places there are strong currents where it flows very rapidly. At times My children experience the strong current of My Spirit. In other places, My stream meanders and hardly seems to be moving at all. Many of My children enjoy these quieter contemplative meandering places.

You My child are in My stream of Kingdom life. You have been in it for many years. Trust that wherever you are, in the strong current or in the quieter meandering place; you are in the stream of My Kingdom of life.

Flowing with you for ever,

Father

Putting Down Roots

Job 29:19; Jeremiah 17:8; John 15:5

My child,

Feelings are not the same as knowing. Feelings are like the leaves on a tree. They are blown this way and that way by the wind. One moment the sun shines on them and they gleam brightly in the sun. But then when darker times come they shrivel up and fall from the tree.

But knowing is like the roots of the tree. They drive deep down into the soil. From here all the goodness and sustenance is drawn up. It is this sustenance from deep down that will support the leaves and their growth.

You see knowing is the rest you have in Me. As I am not only around you but in you and through you. That's why some of My children, who are called 'mystics', emphasise the knowing. That is to put your roots deep down in to Me. And to rest in that knowledge. Can a leaf do anything to sustain itself? No of course not! But the roots draw up all that is needed. So it is with knowing Me deep within. Remember this is by My infinite grace I lavish on you and the faith I give you.

So relax; do not fret. And if your feelings are blowing all over the place in the wind, just smile at this adversity, as you quietly dwell in the inner knowledge you have in Me.

For you are rooted in Me,

Father

Living within You

John 1:1-3; Colossians 1:27

My child

So you wonder where in you I live. You say to yourself, 'does God live in just the electrical activity of my brain?' Or does God live in my 'soul' as some might say? Some say that I, 'the Lord', dwell in your heart.

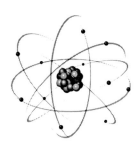

However, let us say you were reduced to the smallest particle in your body, the atom. Well, even the atom and the sub-atomic particles in the atom would have Me in them. Because you are 'in Christ' and 'Christ is in you'. We live in every part of you, my child. Even the electrons contain my presence. There is no part of you that does not contain My presence.

But when your body dies and all that electrical activity in your brain ceases, and you stop thinking even then you will still be in Me, and I will be in you.

For I existed before any material or anything physical existed. I live outside time and space. Yet I also live within and through the universe. And so right now, I live in you. Yes in every part of you. So relax in the awesome truth of My presence. And yet also the down to earth truth that I am your loving heavenly Father who lives in you and through you, by My Spirit.

My presence is hugging you from within,

Father

Let Go and Push Out

John 8:36

My children,

Picture a boat tied up in a harbour all safe  ocean. They are not meant to be tied up in a harbour all the time.

Quite often you as my children stay tied up safely in the harbour. You need to let go and move out in to the freedom I have for each one of you. Stop holding on to where you are. Be adventurous and move out into all I have for you.

Your releasing,

Father

Multitudinous Cuddles

Isaiah 40:11; Hebrews 5:12

My child,

There are times when you still don't really trust Me. Particularly in times of quiet, when I don't appear to be speaking. You feel at these times as if the relationship has broken down and you are at fault.

But don't lovers sometimes lay in each other's arms with not a word being spoken. Yet there is a real communication of love and acceptance, between them. You must learn to rest in My arms of love, and accept that sometimes I won't speak any words. I don't need to always keep speaking to you, for  you have passed the baby stage of having to be spoon fed. You can just sit back, with My arms around you, bathed in My redeeming love. Just trust Me and also trust yourself in My Son Jesus. So relax; words will come but for now rest in My arms of love.

With multitudinous cuddles,

Father

A Smoking Candle

Isaiah 42:3; Luke 11:36

My child,

Remember you looked at a flickering and smoking candle. Often your life burns steady and clear with the life of My Son and My light within it. But there are times when this life flickers and smoke comes forth. These are not good or peaceful periods. But I am continually working within you and some of the things in your life are being burnt off. At these times you are like a flickering flame and there may be some smoke. But note well My son, the flame does not go out or even diminish. It merely flickers and smokes. So is your life as I do My work in you, painful or at least uncomfortable for you? – yes! But do remember the flame never really diminishes does it?

So I am with My child, despite your feelings or lack of them. Despite the flicker of the flame and the smoke; My life continues in you; My light still burns within you.
Just trust and remember the flame never extinguishes, My child.

Illuminatingly,

Father

Chapter 3

Grey Days

Most of us have difficult days or seasons when we are low. However often, those of us who say we trust God and have faith in Him, don't like to admit this. The writer to the Hebrew Christians points out that Jesus was fully human. Therefore he knows what it is like when we feel emotionally low or in some cases stressed.

The writers of the Psalms were prepared to express their raw feelings before God. Eugene Peterson is the author of the Message translation. This translation is very 'down to earth'. He was lead to write this when he was pastor of a church. People would come to him and express that they were struggling or feeling low. He would suggest they went away and read some of the Psalms. However when we read the Psalms in the beautiful Tudor English of the King James Bible, we may not grasp their rawness. This led him to first translate the Psalms and let these be seen in their down to earth and rawness.

When we are low, struggling or just upset with life, we can try and pretend that everything is ok. We may push these thoughts down into our lives and try and bury them. This is not a good idea! Or we may let these thoughts or anger pour out all over our family and friends. Again this is not very helpful. Perhaps one of the best approaches is that expressed by the Psalmists. In the seclusion away from others, in the quietness of our own space, we can express our true feelings, even if negative, to God. Then we can discern His loving response in your heart.

When I first started journaling I was struggling from time to time from depression. I learnt to express these feelings to God. He communicated His love and healing in my heart, in reply. So these letters may lift your hearts as you see his love in the midst of 'grey days'.

Sitting in Darkness

Micah 7:8; Romans 5:3-5

My depressed and suffering child,

I know how hard it is for you to sit in darkness and not to hear My voice. To have no certainty of My Love in your heart. Yet you hang on and that pleases Me. You do not feel it at the moment but I do love you. I do understand how you feel, for My Son hung in the darkness on a cross separated from feeling and knowing My Love. I never stopped loving Him though, even when He descended into the place of departed spirits. On the third day I raised Him from death to life, (with great rejoicing in My Heart and in heaven). It took Him a little while to recover in His risen life, (for remember He wouldn't let Mary touch Him when she came too close in the garden). So too, I will raise you from this present darkness of death to life.

You ask why? But I will never give satisfactory answers to those questions in your life on earth. But often when I allow these things to happen, it is the lessons that are learnt that are important. One lesson I am trying to teach you at the moment is to depend entirely on Me. I have stripped away all human support in terms of satisfying your soul and spiritual needs. (Don't turn this into a doctrine, for you are part of the Body of Christ and need each other.) But at this time I want you to depend entirely on Me.

Let Me restore you to the place of grace. Trust Me, not others. Also be patient, this takes time. Don't worry about the things going on around you. Forget about trying to sort it all out. Let Me sort it out. Just trust that I will do that, without necessarily involving you. Even if you don't think the things around you are right, leave them all in My hands and care, little one. For now let My love and grace flow in your life. Let it grow; Let it flow. Just accept it and carry on with the things you have to hand.

Your loving and understanding,

Father

Tiredness

Matthew 8:23-26; Philippians 4:13

Dear child,

My Son too became tired and weary, but it never stopped His ministry. He always looked to Me for inner strength, and so can you.

Don't ever say, I can't do it. Rather say, with God on my side I will succeed. Don't doubt what I have given you, and don't sit back either. Rather, with hope, look forward with Me; to what I can do through you. But you can relax. It is OK to take a rest now and again. Keep listening to Me and following My direction as My Son did.

Your understanding,

Father

Dull Moments

Numbers 6:24-26; Matthew 17:2

My child,

It may be dull and overcast at the moment but the sun is still giving light and life, above the clouds. So it is in your life, it may be dull at the moment but My Son is giving life to you. Don't look at the outward things, but allow the inner life of My Son to shine through you.

Yours shining upon you,

Father

Truth and Reality

Philippians 1:6; Hebrews 12:1-2

My wondering child,

You still wonder whether you come up to my standards. Are you good enough? Have you done the right things? I have to go on reminding you, patiently and gently, that I accept you fully in Jesus. You were accepted right from the start when you chose My Son as your saviour and Lord. You weren't accepted because you were good enough but because Jesus died on the cross for you. Since then, although My grace has been working in your life and you have changed, you are *still* accepted by Me fully because of My Son's finished work on the cross. I don't accept you on the basis of whether you are good enough, but by My grace.

However, I do take great delight in your recent steps of faith and desire to hear My voice more clearly. These things do not determine your acceptance by Me, but they enrich our relationship.

I know you still wonder whether these things are real and whether you are making them up. It is true that they contain a lot that comes from you; but there is a golden thread of My truth and reality running through them. They are at their centre, what I am saying.

If you will look to Me, I will help you to hear more clearly. There will be areas where you will have to change your way of viewing things. But remember I am gentle in the area of repentance, with My beloved children. So relax in My Love. Accept that I am extremely patient. And remember these are all aspects of eternity that we are dealing with.

So press on and you will receive the prize that waits for you and all My children who pursue the Kingdom with steadfastness and determination.

Yours as ever communicating,

Father

Freedom

Zechariah 4:6; Zephaniah 3:17; Galatians 5:1

My suffering child,

Like the bear you are beginning to walk in your new freedom. I have broken the chains that bound you. The last few links may still be hanging in place but their restraining power is broken. They only serve to remind you of the work I have done in your life. So you can sing:

> *You have broken chains that bound me,*
> *You've set this captive free;*
> *I will lift my voice to praise Your name*
> *For all eternity[1]*

You are beginning to take the first few steps and these are a little unsteady because you're not used to it, yet. But keep moving forward, don't let others stop you or hold you back. Press forward. Let Me do all the hard work! Remember, 'Not by might, nor by power, but by My Spirit', is the key. So press on, with My songs of deliverance ringing in your ears.

Your delivering,

Father

---

[1] Carl Tuttle. Copyright © 1982 Mercy/Vineyard Publishing/Adm. by CopyCare..

Setting you free

John 8:32; John 8:36; Galatians 5:1

My dear child,

I am with you and I know all about you. I see the difficulties you experience and how these cause you to feel down. But in Me you will overcome all the devices of the enemy, wherever they come from.

Stand fast and hold the ground, the ground I have given you, the ground right at your feet. Continue to look to Me and draw upon My Strength.

Above all, trust Me, for I look after you. I continue to set your feet upon the rock. Don't allow the enemy to deceive you with his lies. We set you free, and if the Son sets you free, you are free indeed. Accept you are free in Jesus, and live in that freedom. Let the new patterns of life begin to emerge. Don't worry about the future or dwell in the past. Let Me live through you now and for evermore.

Your ever present,

Father

Dealing with Grey Clouds

2 Samuel 22:29; Isaiah 43:2

My child,

Why fret over the things you cannot seem to do, when in Me and My Son, you can do all things? The feelings you experience are part of your emotional make up, but they do not determine *what* you are and *who* you are. They are like passing clouds. Sometimes such clouds bring rain! But then the sun breaks through and blue skies are over you. Come wind, come rain or even sunshine; you are the same. In Me you are secure. Don't look at the grey clouds over you; rather look at Me and My Son. Let the Holy Spirit move in your life.

Remember it is by faith not by sight that you walk. I will answer your questions. But first you and I need to learn to walk together. You need to cultivate the ability to listen to Me, come hell or high water! For it is from hell that the negative voices come and the pressure, is from the fallen world in which you live. Yes, you are an inexperienced child in My Kingdom, but I have a special place in My Heart for young ones.

Just keep on walking. Trust Me that it will all work out. Not necessarily in the way you imagine, but in a way that brings glory to Me and satisfaction to you. Look up, my child, and I will grant you the desires of your heart.

Your understanding,

Father

Freedom from the Law

Psalm 139:8(KJV); Galatians 5:18

My confused child,

I am with you wherever you go. Even if you make your bed in hell, I will be with you. For I am in you and through you, in My Spirit. Stop worrying about what to do and not to do. Learn to look to Me and not your feelings.

Remember, because of My grace you are free. Not free to sin, but free from keeping the law, including the unwritten laws of your distorted thinking and false expectations. So relax in the freedom that My Son Jesus has brought you through His death and resurrection. Continue to rest in Me, My child. Go in My name, for I am with you, forever more.

Lovingly,

Father

Looking Ahead with Hope

Hebrews 12:2

My child,

Consider My Son. He didn't worry about the future. For the hope set before him, He was prepared to endure the pain of the cross. He immersed himself in My love, My joy and My Spirit. Is He not your example?

Do not feel this is far above you or an unreachable goal. For My Spirit is within you, to strengthen you and guide you, as you walk with Us. Do not look at what you are and where you have come from, (except as a testimony to My grace in you). Rather look ahead with hope, for the joy that is set before you in My Son, Jesus. Straight is the path before you, and your feet are firmly on this path, even if they feel a little shaky at this stage. So enjoy the journey. I do.

Your guiding heavenly Father

Do Not Strive

Psalm 119:11; Isaiah 61:10

My child,

Why do you worry about things? Remember, I have put My word within your heart. Also remember, 'you are you!' I created you in your inner most being. Remember the mould was perfect even if the casting was flawed. But I am removing the flaws and healing the hurts. Let Me work these things out in your life. Do not strive, but relax into them. I see your sin, but I forgive it. I clothe you in the righteousness of Jesus.

Yours in all the circumstances of your life,

Father

Not By Sight

2 Corinthians 5:7

My child

Do remember you walk by faith and not by sight. Why do you keep looking for some experience before you will accept that I am really working in you. Faith is trusting in Me when you cannot see Me or hear My voice. Faith is trusting that I am at work in you, even when you don't have tingles down your spine, or goose bumps on your arms. Faith is total trust in Me, without any physical evidence.

But be assured, I am in you and you are in Me. This has been brought about through your faith in Me. It is still brought about by your daily faith in Me. So trust Me. Don't look for physical manifestations or spiritual experiences. If they come, rejoice and praise Me for them. If they don't, continue to worship Me and praise Me and so live your life of faith. Remember, I am at work in you. I will use you. Just trust Me, day by day.

With heavenly confidence,

Father

Holiness

John 12:47; Romans 6:14

My suffering child,

Why do you make such a thing about how you feel? Why do you make such an issue over your church? It is Me that you should be focusing on, not on these other things. Your hope is built in Me, not in them. Even if the world and all that is in it passed away, you would still be secure in Me.

You are also too hard on yourself. Accept yourself as I do. No you are not perfect but I take delight in you as a child. You may not be demonstrating what you know in your heart yet; but let it come from within. Relax. Don't strive. Don't accept rules and regulations. Don't let life consist of 'I must do this, or even I must be more loving'. Let Me bring forth that which I have already put in you and I will continue to help it grow.

Remember holiness is an area for you to concentrate on. But don't make it heavy, or other-worldly or difficult. Holiness is being in Me and I in you, through the Spirit. Learn to meditate on Me. Learn to 'be still' in the presence of Me, (your Lord and heavenly 'dad').

As for the church you may be right, occasionally, in your reaction to it. Don't take that to mean that I condemn the church. Remember I love churches even when they have problems and faults. (Remember Corinth!)

Sometimes one person may not fit in a particular church. This doesn't imply judgement, criticism or sin. It only highlights that My children are all different and unique. My children like you are hopefully always in the process of change. (After all salvation is an on-going activity.) So at particular times, My children may not fit into one particular church.

At such times they need to listen to Me even more clearly and let Me lead them either to stay in that church or out of it. But do relax. Please don't worry. After all I never do!

With much love, your ever present,

Father

In the Pit

2 Samuel 3:25(KJV); Psalm 139:8(KJV); Daniel 10:25; Hebrews 13:5

My child

I know all your ins and outs; all your comings and goings; nothing is hidden from My sight. Do you really think I have forsaken you? Can you not recall My promise that, 'I will never leave you nor forsake you'.

True, you are in a pit of depression but I am there with you. Even if 'you made your bed in hell', I would be with you. You cannot run away from My presence. Although you may place yourself outside the benefits of My blessings of grace, when you refuse to rest in My inner presence, within you.

Do not fear the way ahead. For I am with you My child. Just trust Me, even when the going is difficult. I have heard your prayers and I will answer them, in due course. So relax and rest and trust in Me.

Yours as always, even in your dark days,

Father

Pressing On

Leviticus 19:18; Matthew 6:12; Romans 8:11

My little one,

You are My child and I am your Father, patient one. I know all your ins and outs, your ups and downs. I am not displeased with you, for you are growing in grace. True yours has been a slow growth in grace, but then much of your learning, like some of My children, is slow. But at the same time it is deep and true. So don't give up. Don't despair over the difficulties. You are very close to My heart. Continue to learn to be kind to yourself. Don't judge others harshly, for I don't. I love you with a precious, gentle and everlasting love.

Be free in My love. Let the Spirit flow in and through you. Do trust Me in all you do, say and think. For I am with you, (through My Spirit); I am for you and I am on your side. I want the best for you, my little one.

Don't look at others in terms of comparison. You are unique, just as they are. Only look with the eyes of compassion on others. Rejoice in their triumphs and strength. Forgive and accept them in their weaknesses; just as I have forgiven you all your debt, through the death of My Son on the cross.

Through the Spirit, I pour into you the same power that raised Him from death to life, so that you will be raised continually from death to life. Press on My child, looking to Jesus who has gone before. Be filled with My Spirit day by day.

Your ever caring,

Father

Following God's Plan

Psalm 37:5(KJV); Isaiah 30:21

My child,

Whatever you do or wherever you turn, I am with you. You long to know what you should do. But you are already doing the most important thing, which is to turn to Me through your faith in Jesus. I don't always show the way with 'large flashing lights'. Sometimes I trust My children to move in the right direction through what their minds and spirits indicate. If the direction is completely wrong then My Spirit will indicate this through a feeling of spiritual uneasiness or a lack of peace.

Remember My plan for your life can cope with a few kinks and deviations caused by a few short-term wrong choices. Often My children grow more through these times of difficulty than they do in the days of great certainty over the plans for their lives. So rejoice; give thanks; for I am with you and will continue to watch over your life. Commit your ways to Me and I will guide you in the choices you make.

With My guiding hand,

Father

Close to His Heart

Psalm 73:26; Acts 15:8

Oh My child!

Why do you think I would ever cast you away?   Do you still not realise how much I love you? Do not try to work out this love with your mind. Rather let your heart open up to receive it. Receive it in the same way that a child receives a parent's love. Just let yourself be enveloped in My arms of love.   Let Me hold you up close to My beating heart of love.

Let the name of Jesus be on your lips. For He is the greatest expression of My love. His death should remind you to what extent I love you. Open up your heart to My love. Rejoice in My Son Jesus. Flow in My Holy Spirit. Above all learn to enjoy Me as I minister to you. Then let Me begin to flow out from you to others. For I am always with you.

With much love,

'Abba' Father

Being Filled with My Spirit

2 Corinthians 4:17(KJV); Ephesians 5:18

My child,

I will fill you with My Spirit. Do you really think I would overlook you? Never! For you are My child and are called by My name. Don't rely on your feelings when it comes to moving in the Spirit. Rather rely on the inner promptings that come from Me.

Above all, by faith, trust that you are in Me and I am in you. Accept that you are accepted. Know that you are forgiven and cleansed in the blood of My Son Jesus. Trust that My Spirit is moving in your life.

Yes, I know your faults and all your weaknesses. But My treasure has always been contained in earthen vessels. However, I am at work in you, redeeming and changing you through My Love. Continue to look to Me. Set your heart and desire on My Kingdom, first and foremost in your life. Let My Spirit renew your mind and its thinking. Do continue to relax in My love.

Accept that I am with you always, wherever you go. That includes the place where you work. Enjoy My company for I enjoy yours. For I am yours forever and ever, world without end.

As ever with abundant love,

Father

My Presence Surrounds You

1 Kings 19:11-12; John 9:5

My child,

Why have you sat in silence, when My voice is all around you. Why have you sat in darkness when the light of My presence surrounds you? My voice is rarely still and I seldom hide my light from view. The reason I seem not to be speaking is that you have closed the ears of your heart. The reason you do not see is because your spiritual eyes are shut. It is the enemy that spread's lies. It is he that deceives you, so that you think I am silent and hidden from view.

Like Elijah take the steps that lead you out of the cave. Then you will be in the place where I can speak to you, in My still small voice. There I will be able to show you things you need to see. Do not strive to bring this about. All you need are the steps of faith. To take one step at a time as you walk by faith, and not by human sight. Allow Me to fill your heart with joy and peace through My Spirit. Remember Jesus is himself your peace.

For now just trust that I am in you and you are in Me, through My Son Jesus and the work of My Spirit. Whilst you may be encouraged by other Christians, don't try to be like them. I have made you the way you are. True the person I meant you to be was damaged by the things you experienced, especially in your childhood years. Your character has also been flawed by the sin of the wrong choices you have made. But remember, My on-going work of grace in your life. I am healing the hurts, washing away the sins and breaking the things that bind you. My wholeness is beginning to emerge in your life. Do continue to look forward with the hope that comes from Me. Do expect Me to guide you and lead you on. Though remember I don't always do things the way you expect. And yes I can and I will use you. Just use the opportunities I give you, small though they may seem at times.

Remember, as you serve Me, walk by faith. That is trust that I am at work in you and working through you, in these opportunities. And of course remember that all you do at 'work, rest or play' is part of the life of faith. As ever I remain the eternal Word and the true light of the world.

Tenderly,

Father

In Periods of Sadness

John 11:35; Hebrews 4:15

My sorrowful child,

I do understand how you feel. Remember, Jesus lived as a human being and experienced such emotions, including sadness. You will come through this period. I see how you try to 'hang on' by reading the Bible. But even if you gave up on your activities towards Me, I wouldn't. For underneath you are indeed the everlasting arms. You see you just can't run away from Me, or fall out of My love.

I do have your life and future in My hands. Trust Me in all things. Both the small and big things. I will show you the way ahead, but do be patient. For now relax in the knowledge that I love you, even if you cannot feel this at the moment. Don't worry about feelings or thoughts. Just relax in your trust and knowledge that I love you and will never let you go.

For I remain yours and through all the ages,

Father

Listen to the Stillness

*Written a few days after the author's father had died.
Sitting in the beautiful and peaceful grounds of Lee Abbey in North Devon, UK*

Ephesians 2:14

My child,

Listen to the stillness broken only by the birds singing in the trees. Sit in this place of deep peace. Remember My peace that is Jesus Himself. Your father who has just died is now in this peace. You too can enjoy My peace. Rest your heart in Me. Turn off all your restless thoughts. Just dwell in My kingdom and sit in the peace of this place. Let my stillness, still your heart. Do continue to rest in Me. Together we will walk forward in the kingdom of life and peace. Together we will face any troubles or sadness that comes to you. I am in you and you are in Me, through My Son Jesus.

Your ever caring,

Father

Grey Days

Face the Future with Hope

Psalm 25:21; Psalm 118:24(KJV); Ephesians 6:14

My child,

In your heart you know of My eternal love for you. I do see how you struggle to know and feel this love. You must know how I value all you do for Me. I see your faithfulness and determination to serve Me. Believe Me, I know your faults and sin before you commit them. But they do not drive away My love for you. No, rather My love and care for you grows, just like that of a good parent. I want you to grow in my love. I want you to overcome your weaknesses. I want you to move out into an area of more wholeness in your life. I see how you are seeking that and it brings a smile to My face.

Remember you are too hard on yourself at times. Do learn to love yourself just as I love you. Turn to Me in repentance and your sins are forgiven, and you are cleansed from them. Indeed I clothe you with the righteousness of Jesus, as you put on the breastplate of righteousness. Relax, enjoy the day before you. Face the future with hope.

Yours as ever and with you constantly,

Father

Feelings are Fickle

2 Corinthians 5:7 (KJV)

My child,

I do hear the cry of your heart to know Me and My Son Jesus more intimately. But do understand you are as close to My heart as you can get. I know you want to be more conscious of being filled with the Spirit. You also desire to know the joy of the Lord.

But remember you walk by faith and not by feelings. Feelings are fickle things, here today and gone tomorrow. Faith is a firm foundation. It is trusting Me in all situations, no matter what you are feeling.

But it is My delight to pour My blessings upon you. It gives Me great joy to lavish My grace upon you. Just trust that you are in Me through Jesus. Continue to trust that I am in you through my Spirit. Step out in faith. Just trust Me when you speak to others. Accept that I am with you when you speak to people or pray for them, such as at meetings.

As you continue to put your trust in Me, particularly when you worship Me, I will cause joy to rise up in your heart. Feelings will follow faith, just trust Me on that one.

Continue to read the Bible and to speak in tongues. But remember these are not works to gain my favour; rather they are vehicles of My grace. My life can flow as you read My word and prayer, particularly in tongues. So press on in faith.

Yours intimately,

Father

The Apple of His Eye

Deuteronomy 32:10; Zechariah 2:8; Philippians 4:13

My child,

What if in your eyes you were a failure? What if you thought you couldn't do anything? Would these be true? For in Jesus you are precious in My sight. You are always the 'apple of My eye'. I take great delight in you at all times. Remember in Jesus My Son you can do all things.

But now is a fallow time. Remember in winter the ground lies dormant. Often it has frost on its surface, and cold winds blow over it. But then in the spring, shoots begin to appear. The sun shines on the earth and it is watered by the gentle spring rains. Then the plants shoot ahead. Flowers and fruit begin to appear in abundance.

You are at a quiet place. But new things will come. Oh how I love you. It grieves Me when you cannot receive it or accept it. But it is true My child, I love you with an endless love.

Let My truth, who is Jesus My Son, supplant the misbeliefs and lies. Receive Jesus who is Himself your peace. Rest, do not strive. Let My Spirit flow from within you. Let it flow; let it grow. Forgive yourself and accept yourself as I do, through Jesus. Be kind to yourself. Accept your limitations. Do not try to do everything; receive my love; receive My rest in My acceptance of you.

Yours as ever and for ever,

Father

Open the Door of Faith

2 Corinthians 5:7(KJV); Ephesians 1:7-8

My child,

You are growing stronger. This is not purely through self-effort but through the strengths I am building into you. I know recently you have had some difficult times. But you have met these and come through them and out the other side.

But do remember faith is an active word. It is not like an automatic door that just opens when you approach it. You need to take the steps of faith. Remember you walk by faith and not by sight. You need to walk forward and open the door by faith. This means you have to give a gentle push to the door in faith. If it is My doorway, then through faith it will swing open. Occasionally the door might not open, maybe because it is not the right time for you to go through it.

Above all keep a lightness in your spirit. Don't worry about things or what other people think. Just keep looking to Me and put your trust in Me.

For I remain committed to you and your family. Remember I love to lavish My grace upon you. Continue to look to Me through My word. Feed upon it constantly. Open your heart to Me in prayer. Listen to my voice constantly. Enjoy my endless love. On the days that are bleak and black, just trust that My love like the sunshine will break through in time.

For I remain your affectionate,

Father

Looking Forward with Hope

Isaiah 43:7; 2 Corinthians 12:10; Ephesians 2:10

My child

I have made you the way you are. Do not feel ashamed of how you feel. You are unique like all of My children. True, when you came from My mould you were not whole and complete as I intended. There were large areas of brokenness. But over the years My redeeming love has healed many of the hurts and restored much that was lost. Learn to be yourself. Don't be apologetic about who you are. But equally do not be arrogant or proud and look down on others. You are My child and I take great delight in you. Continue to serve Me. For this brings great joy to My heart. I know you have felt your weakness and felt very fragile at times. But you have pressed on and served Me and others. You have no idea how much this has 'knocked Me out'! So just relax and hear My 'well done son'. I will continue to use you. These testing times are teaching you more of Me. For instance you have learnt how My strength is made real within the midst of your weakness. Look forward with hope, to the way I will use you and your wife. Go forward with My songs of deliverance ringing in your ears.

Eternally yours,

Father

The Way Ahead is Open

Zechariah 4:6; 2 Corinthians 4:7(KJV)

My child,

See the way ahead is open before you. It is not a difficult or rough road. And remember, each journey starts a step at a time. So take this first step. Again remember, you walk by faith and not by sight. I would remind you, that it is not by might, not by power but by my Spirit, that you live child.

Do not be afraid. Let My hope fill your soul. Let My love melt your heart. Trust Me child. There really is no alternative. But I just love it when My children choose to trust Me. To trust Me, even when the way ahead is not clear. Believe Me; I do have a future and a hope for all My children. All I ask is that you take this first step with trust and hope in Me.

I have heard your cries to be filled with My Spirit. I just love it when you say, 'more Lord'. I also see your need for more joy in your heart. You have already received and experienced a large measure of this new life and freedom. Look at the way you have more energy to get on with things. Look at how, less and less things do not cause you any hassle or stress.

It is true that you are not perfect or whole yet. But a great truth is that this new life in the Spirit is contained in earthen vessels. Rejoice more. Learn to have more freedom in praise. If only My children could see the joy in My heart when I hear their praise and worship. So go forth in joy with My eternal songs of deliverance and freedom ringing in your ears.

Your ever caring, ever sharing,

Father

Grey Days

Intimacy
('Throne room)

Hebrews 4:16

During a conference called 'Sitting at the feet of Jesus' one of the speakers shared a picture the Lord had given him. This was that he was in the 'throne room' of God. People were looking in from outside the door. The Lord said to the speaker, 'why don't they come in?' One night when the author couldn't sleep not long after this conference, these words came to him. Later the author turned it into a song.

Sometimes I sit and I wonder
Sometimes a dryness I feel
I wonder what I am missing
My emptiness I reveal.

> *And I'm sitting at Jesus' feet*
> *Real intimacy we share*
> *There in the Father's throne room*
> *Jesus righteousness I wear.*

Sometimes I stand in the doorway
Look at this place of delight
'My child why don't you enter?'
Are Your words of welcome and light.

> *And I'm sitting...*

Sometimes I enter in confidence
Your call for me to draw near
A lightness I feel in my spirit
And Your love overcomes all my fear

> *And I'm sitting...*

Disturbing Winds

Romans 8:38-39

My child,

Your feet are truly standing firm on the rock who is Jesus My Son. The shoes of the gospel of peace are on your feet. The shoes of 'shalom' or wholeness provide a firm footing for you in Jesus.

But even though your feet are firm you may still be shaken by strong winds or by storms. True sometimes the wind of My Spirit may shake you. This is normally a gentle shaking. It is more like swaying in the wind. It might lead to a change of direction in life. But because these come from Me the source of life, they are life-filled and liberating. They are never destructive.

However, you may also experience some storms swirling around you. These will often come from the turbulent and fallen world you live in. They can be very disturbing. But if your feet are truly gripping the rock who is Jesus then they will not destroy you. It is also true that the enemy may also send his storms to swirl around you. But these are usually of doubt and lies. You know, My child, the answer to all of these is in and through Jesus; who is the way the truth and the life. You also know that you only have to say 'boo' in Jesus' name and the enemy will slink away like a pathetic weak cat. All the signs of the roaring lion vanish when you speak in the authority and power of Jesus' name.

Oh yes, and let's for a moment think of the disturbing breezes of emotional difficulties. These are not such a big issue really. Provided you continue to remember that when you are 'in Christ' you are also in Me. Your position is that you are held in My arms of love close to My chest. There you should realise that you are close to My heart of love for you. At each beat it says: 'I love you; I like you; I fully accept you; you are My dearest child'. And finally it continually says, 'nothing can or will ever separate you from Me, My child'.

I do know that you sometimes struggle with your emotions as do many of My children. (Though they rarely share this fact with their fellow brothers and sisters!) But remember Jesus is himself your shalom. He is your peace. He is your wholeness; your healing; your completeness and your restoration.

So let's laugh together when the winds, wherever they come from, swirl around you.

Yours constantly,

Father

Be Who You Are

Romans 8:29; 2 Corinthians 4:7

Child,

Why try to be what you are not? Instead be who you are! Be who you are in Me. Remember My treasure is contained in an earthen, that is imperfect, vessel. But I your Father live in you, through Jesus My Son and the work of My Spirit. So don't strive to be like others or even try to emulate them.

Just rest in Me and let Me transform your life, to the image of Me in your life. It will be My image that comes through the true you. We will together, by My gentle and loving grace, continue to bring more wholeness into some broken areas of your life. Will there always be some small cracks or flaws in the vessel that will show? Yes, but they will be fading all the time as you allow the sense of My inner presence within you to heal and transform you.

So relax; so rest in Me; allow Me to work within and through you.

Gently and with patience,

Father

Shalom

During a Foundation in Leadership course the speaker mentioned the Hebrew word shalom. This word, usually translated as peace, also has roots of salvation, wholeness, richness, completeness etc... This inspired me to write this song. A song that is very appropriate for a 'Grey Day'.

The healing fountain flows;
Shalom the wholeness grows.
Within our hearts Lord;
Within our hearts Lord.
Let it grow; Let it flow;
For all eternity.

The crystal water clear,
It banishes our fear.
Within our hearts Lord;
Within our hearts Lord.
Let it grow; Let it flow;
For all eternity.

And Lord Your hope is here,
That Jesus shall appear.
Within this world Lord;
Within this world Lord.
Peace begun; Let Him come;
Now and for evermore.

Chapter 4

Everlasting Love

Ever since the beginning of creation, God has been declaring His love towards it. Implicit in this is His love for people. This love is not a transitory affair of, 'here today and gone tomorrow'. Through Jeremiah, who is often thought of as a rather gloomy prophet, He said:

> *'I have loved you with an everlasting love; I have drawn you with unfailing kindness.'*
> Jeremiah 31:3 (NIV).

Paul declares an even more amazing truth that He had us in mind before the creation of the world. For he wrote to the Ephesian Christians:

> *'For he chose us in him before the creation of the world.'*
> Ephesians 1:4

This love is even stronger and truer than any human love, for Isaiah writing to God's people says:

> *'Can a mother forget the baby at her breast and have no compassion on the child she has borne? Though she may forget, I will not forget you!'*
> Isaiah 49:15

It is a great shame that so often those of us who have come to know Him through Jesus, fail to appreciate this amazing love of His for us. In many of these letters my heavenly Father whispered in to my heart of His love. Hopefully you may realise He is saying the same thing to you.

> 'My children', He is saying to all of us, 'I love you with all My heart for ever'.

Infinite Love

John 3:16

Dear child,

I really do love you. I want you to know, that if you were the only person in the world, I would still send My Son to die for you. You are worth it to Me. Yes, I know how you feel incapable of feeling love, but believe Me, this will change.

You have already changed as My Grace has worked in your life. Just let the gentle dove of My Spirit melt your cold heart. Let Him change you from within. Give Me your heart as well as your mind, and I will live in and through you. Together we will enjoy the Kingdom. Together we will experience the joy and the pain. For Mine is the Kingdom, the power, and the glory. You are meant to experience the result of this.

With much love,

Father

The Greatness of My Kingdom

Matthew 7:1

My child,

I will teach you, but only listen to Me. Judge not and you will not be judged. Lift up your eyes and see the greatness of My Kingdom. Listen to the words of life that I pour over you and learn from Me. For I am gentle, patient and kind. Let the centre of your life be Me; and I will be in all things, through all things, now and for evermore.

Your everlasting,

Father

Heavenly Love

Psalm 89:2

My child,

Remember My love, which comes from heaven itself. It is constant and unchanging; eternal in its origin and destiny. I have chosen to share this love with My children. It is My gift to them. If only they will open up their hearts and receive, I will fill them with My love. It is a free gift that I give in response to their faith.

You cannot earn it and striving won't bring it any closer. Just receive it as part of My grace to you. It is this love you must share with others, including those around you. Your love may fail; mine never will! Your patience may evaporate; mine is eternal, like heaven from which it comes. Learn to receive, learn to share, and I will be with you always.

Father

Fleeting Thoughts

Philippians 4:8, Ephesians 1: 7-8

My struggling child,

A fleeting thought is not sin, but temptation, and we know who is the source of all this! The sin in such thought life, is when you accept the thought and dwell on it. Remember the advice Paul gave:

> *Whatever is true, whatever is noble, whatever is pure, whatever is lovely, whatever is admirable - if anything is excellent or praise worthy - think about such things.*

Learn to think about My Son more often. Think about your position in Him with Me. For you are My adopted son. Let My grace flow over you in all its abundance. Remember to pray at all times and in all places.

Your caring,

Father

God's Care

Psalm 84:3; Matthew 10:29-31

My child,

Why would you think that I don't care about you? Remember My Word says that two sparrows are sold for a farthing, yet not one drops to the ground without Me knowing all about it. So don't be afraid. You are worth more than many sparrows.

I know all about you; I see everything you do and perceive, every thought you think. Despite your weakness and the times you sin, I do not reject you. I love you with an everlasting love. That means it never comes to an end. It never, never ceases. It is un-conditional. Even when you sin; I still love you. True, deliberate sin stops the blessing of My love resting upon you, so that you cannot receive it. But My love never diminishes, nor does it ever grow tired. Learn to accept My love; learn to receive it. Refuse to accept the negative feelings you have.

Don't worry about your relationship with others and how you fit in. (Continue to care about them and allow this love to grow.) Don't worry if you don't conform to those around you. Only learn to conform to being My child and doing those things I have planned for you to do. Don't strive to move in revelation knowledge for others. Rather relax in My love and grace. Just be yourself within the acceptance of My love.

Don't try to meet others expectations for you. Just do your best in My strength. Learn to please Me as your Spiritual Father. (Not that you don't please Me already.) Continue in My grace. Let love fill your heart, even when you struggle with your feelings. My feelings for you are constant. You are never far from My heart, tender one.

Affectionately,

Dad

Glimpses of My Heart

Psalm 41:12 (KJV); Revelation 3:8

My child,

You glimpse My heart. You see what I set before you and I will not take it away. Keep looking to Jesus. I reveal Him more and more to you. You are a prince in My Kingdom; so don't forget it! Let Me fill you again and again with My Spirit. Continue to look to Me and I will supply all your needs.

Your loving Father who is always there

Father of Grace

Isaiah 61:10; Romans 8:23; Ephesians 2:8-9

My little one,

You are right to reject works and to live in Grace through faith. You are declared righteous because My Son died for you; and you have believed. You 'are put right' as you place your trust in Him. Therefore, I have clothed you in Jesus' righteousness. You are My child, adopted into My family, and nothing you can do will earn that position. For I gave it to you when you believed in and accepted Jesus, My Son.

It has taken Me many years to get you to realise this truth. To accept it and live in it. But now you are beginning to move in it. Don't let anyone talk you out of it!

Remember who it is that lies and deceives! Who is it that robs My children of their blessings? It is certainly not Me! I only offer blessings and encouragement to My children, because I love them. So freely receive and freely give. Go in My Peace and serve others.

Your Father of Grace

Letting Go

Psalm 46:4; Ezekiel 47:12

My children,

My loving kindness is like a river which flows without end. Its source is My heart, before time began. Above all it flows through the cross where My Son died for you.

Immerse yourself in My Love. Let it flow over you and through you, so that others may be refreshed by it. By faith let go of the bank and let yourself go with the flow.

Flowing with my love,

Father

Transformation of the mind

Genesis 2:3; Psalm 62:5; Hebrews 4:9

My child,

You are My child and I love you very much. It pleases Me that you want to make a breakthrough in your relationship with Me. I know you still worry about your poor memory and lack of sharpness in your thinking. However, don't worry about these things but continue to seek Me and My face. I will restore your spiritual position, but you must let Me do it in My way and My time.

Be patient, know that I accept you fully in My Son. I love you just as you are at the moment, though My desire is to continue to transform your life, making you more whole. So for the time being relax. By all means continue to read My Word as part of the process. But remember it is we, Father, Son and Holy Spirit, who do all the hard and difficult work. Your part is to accept and cooperate in the process. Peace to you My child.

Your loving,

Father

Precious to Me

Deuteronomy 32:10; 1 Corinthians 13:12

My children

You are called by My name and are precious to Me. For you are 'the apple of My eye'. I take delight in you. For you are My children and I am your Father. I look down the tunnel of eternity, and you are with Me. Not just for now but for eternity.

You only see part of My glory now, but you *will* see Me as I am, fully. So go on with joy in your hearts and filled with all hope, through My Spirit and in My Son.

Eternally yours,

Father

Relax in My Love

Psalm 119:50; Isaiah 53:3; Romans 5:3

My suffering child,

The reason you cannot hear Me is not because I am not speaking, but because when you become low and dispirited you shut out the reception of My voice. I do understand that things have been extremely frustrating for you. There has been very little to encourage you.

I will teach you to cope with such situations. Your strength will come from Me. Remember My Son experienced this lack of encouragement but relied on My strength and My love. Don't look at the things around you. Don't rely on other people. Yes, they are meant to be an encouragement, but they like you, often fail in this area. My Love for you has not diminished and I am not cross with you. So relax in my love.

Your loving,

Father

Adventurers

Psalm 25:5 (KJV); Matthew 6:10; Colossians 1:11

My adventurers,

Be patient. Do learn to wait for Me to act. It may not always be as quickly as you would like. But, it's always in time, My time! My kingdom will come, on earth as it is in heaven, but not necessarily in the timescales that you look for. But, these eternal timescales are divinely perfect.

Learn to wait for Me with expectancy, whilst being patient. I will lead you forward in My own good time.

Your ever patient and loving,

Father

Encouragement

Deuteronomy 1:38; John 19:30; Hebrews 9:14

My adopted child,

You don't have to do anything, My child, for We have done it all for you. You only have to receive the benefits that were won on Calvary by My Son.

We are pleased with you. Why don't you realise this? You look so much for others to affirm you and encourage you. Often they don't. But I will always affirm you and encourage you.

I accept you in Jesus and His finished work. Only have faith My child, only believe. Rather than expecting others to encourage you and affirm you; why not bless *them* with encouragement? We will bless you as you do it. We will show you the way ahead, difficult as it may appear to be. Just relax in My arms, child. Trust Me, your Heavenly Father to look after you.

Encouragingly,

Father

A Plan for your Life

Psalm 20:4; Jeremiah 29:11

My child,

I do have a plan for your life, a plan that suits you perfectly. Do not think that because of the setbacks and difficulties you have missed it. I am bigger than your mistakes. You do not see things from My perspective. Can you see all of the plan, not just for your life, but for the whole universe? True, in a perfect world where you were perfect, it wouldn't have been quite so difficult. But then a perfect world would not have needed My plan of salvation and redemption. You are in a fallen and broken world, so an important part of the plan is to bring salvation into your life.

My healing work is required in you. This does take some time. True you could have speeded up the process if you had made different choices earlier in your life. But I forgive you and there is no condemnation because of them. Also I am patient. I can wait for you. So let Me guide you into My healing and restoring process. Do learn to trust Me. Expect Me to act in accordance with My nature as expressed in My living Word, Jesus. But it won't be in the way you expect it! Nor when you expect it!

Do explore the avenues of healing open to you. Do draw upon My resources. Do let Me transform your mind and thinking. Let My love heal your broken feelings. Because of the cross, I do forgive you. I do understand your lack of feelings. Remember I accept you just as you are. You are Mine and I am yours for ever and ever, world without end.

Your never changing and ever caring,

Father

Lies and Grace

Psalm 40:2; Isaiah 49:16; John 20:25

My child,

There is nothing you can do to win My favour and acceptance. Neither can you earn My blessings. I give them all to you, in Christ, as a gift. That's what Grace is all about. You accepted My offer of life in My Son, Jesus; and so I poured life in My Spirit into you.

Yet you still wonder whether I accept you. You still think, maybe I'm not good enough to be His son. No, in your natural life, you are not good enough; you never were and you never will be! But you were worth My Son dying for you. Now in Him I accept you fully. I see you as perfect-in and through Him. I will never leave you. I will never forsake you. You are engraved on the palms of My hands, remember!

When you accept the lies and deceit the enemy sows, particularly from your old and natural life, you are still accepted. You are still mine. I still love you. But, you lose the benefits and blessing of My gift of life. My heart is saddened whilst you accept and live in the lies. But I will not just pull you out of the pit of despair. You have to choose to turn and live in My truth again. I have to let you learn the lesson of grace. The lessons are worth learning and you are beginning to learn them, even if it has been a painful process.

Remember I love you at all times and in all places. You are mine and I am yours for ever.

Lovingly,

Father

The Father's Heart of Love

1 Kings 9:3; Psalm 33:11; Romans 8:38-39

My child,

You still do not really know My heart of love towards you. True, you do know Me and hear My voice. But now learn to hear My heart. My heart of love towards you and all My children; children who are born of their faith in My Son Jesus.

Look into My eyes by faith, and see the warmth of My love. Open your ears even more to hear My words of love. My Son and His death on the cross demonstrate how deep and how wide such love is. This love is towards you and all who believe. Sometimes the wounds of the past close the door on receiving My love. Sometimes the cares of today and the hurts that are caused, prevent the warmth of My love reaching your heart.

Forget what is past and endure through the hurts of today in order to reach the place where My love and peace reside. Remember nothing can separate you from My love, not even death. So allow the warmth of My love to heal the hurt places. Allow it to mend the broken emotions of the past. Let it banish all fear and drive out uncertainty. Just learn to hear My word to your heart, 'I love you dearly as My child'.

Yours as ever with boundless love,

Father

Always on your Side

Ezekiel 37:9; Psalm 140:7; John 8:44

My child,

You are My delight. How I rejoice over you with My songs of deliverance. The fact that you look to Me as your rock and as your deliverer, fills Me with great joy. It is My delight to stand by you through times of trouble, as well as, rejoicing together in the good times. All through your life I am your deliverer.

I am not remote and far off. I am as close to you as the air you breathe. I am in and through you by My Spirit. I am all around you and go wherever you go. Do you think I would reject you or leave you? May be in your distorted thinking and damaged feelings, you occasionally receive this lie. Because of My faithfulness and My unchanging nature, I am always there. I am always on your side and by your side. You only have to turn from such distorted thinking and open the doors of your heart and My love and presence will flood in.

Just learn to trust in Me more and more. Learn to reject the distortion and lies that the enemy sowed in your life in the past and still whispers in your ears today. Learn to hear My gentle and life giving voice. Look to Jesus My Son in whom you see a true and undistorted image of Me. Continue to open up your spirit to My holy and life-giving Spirit, for I remain as ever your loving and unchanging,

Eternal Father

My Outstretched Arms of Love

John 15:13; Romans 5:5

My children,

Stand beneath my cross. Stand beneath my outstretched arms of love. See how wide is My love and how all embracing it is. Look into My eyes and see what depth of acceptance is there. Open up your hearts to My heart. My heart that beats with love. When you meet together, let your voices and music join together; for I am there in the midst of it.

Flooding Your Heart with Peace

Psalm 24:8; 2 Corinthians 8:9; 1 John 4:8

My child,

Just hold this in your heart, that I want you to become rich. Rich in the things I give you. For I long to lavish My grace upon you. I long for My Spirit to flood your heart with love, My love. For I am love. Infinite, unconditional, incomprehensible, unfathomable love. And I direct this towards you My child, because My Son Jesus became poor, even to death on the cross. I long to flood your heart with peace, as Jesus My son is himself your peace.

So open up the door of your heart and let the King of Glory come in. With Him comes, love, grace, peace and even much more heavenly treasure. Remember I have loved you with an everlasting love, and still love you immensely today.

With great affection,

Father

Rest in My Presence

Psalm 23:2; Psalm 119:109

My child,

Rest in My presence. Remember, you don't need to do anything. You don't need to think it all out. Give your brain a rest! Relax in Me. Trust, I am there right with you. I know how your feelings let you down. But even when you don't feel My presence, I am there right with you. But do trust that the feelings will come, in due course. Where you walk, I walk beside you. When you speak, I can give you the words, the words of life. But you need to trust Me. You also need the flow of the Spirit of love in your heart, so that your words may be gracious and healing.

You so often want to know what to do. But so often I put the opportunities before you. Trust that I have given these to you. Just put your hand to it and do it. Trust that I am there with you. Don't worry about feelings. Don't ask yourself did I do this right. Do you think I don't know your funny little ways! And remember I accept you just as you are. I can use you, as you trust Me and get on with things. Even if you sometimes think this is my idea! Do you not think I might have given it to you, without you knowing. So relax My child and trust Me.

Everlastingly,

Father

Throughout the Ages

Proverbs 18:15 (KJV); John 13:35

My restless child,

Do not fret yourself over what you believe. You believe in Me and My Son Jesus. You find yourself in Me by Grace. This means there is nothing you can do to earn My favour, or acceptance. My everlasting love flows constantly like a river. All you need to do is to place yourself in its flow. Or as My word says, open the ears and eyes of your heart.

Do not worry if others don't see things as you see them. Equally understand that to them, they don't always understand or agree with you. But open up a heart filled with love for all My children. Remember as you show love to one another, (despite the differences); the world will come not only to know you are My followers, but will see the witness of My love for the world. But your love for your brothers and sisters is not exclusive; remember to love your neighbours also. To the question who is my neighbour, Jesus showed it was everyone, including ones enemies.

Remember, love is the greatest thing in the world. In particular, I loved the whole world enough, to send Jesus to die for all the people who are in the world, who have ever been in the world, or will be in the world in the future. So continue to stand in the stream of My love.

Throughout all the ages I remain yours,

Father

Accept My Acceptance

Psalm 46:10; Psalm 121:8; Matthew 10:8

My child,

I know you're coming in and you're going out. All your ways are known to Me and nothing is hidden from my sight. Whether you are rejoicing on the mountain top in the bright sunshine, close to my face; or down in the mist covered gorge, where I seem to be hidden from sight; I am with you. My voice is never still, it is always speaking. Sometimes I speak without using words. For I speak through the things around you. The sun on your face. The wind rustling the leaves in the trees. The green grass and vegetation, and the birds singing their songs of praise to Me. These all speak of Me.

But I do speak to your heart. Usually it is the whisper of My words of love. To hear them you need to still yourself. You need to block out the lies and deceit of the enemy. You need also to 'tune out' the restlessness of your own heart and emotions. Be still and know that I am God. Be still and receive My Love, which is an everlasting love. Do not accept the lies and deceit that may come from within you or from external sources. I would particularly say to you the following words:

> *Accept My acceptance.*
> *Feel My forgiveness.*
> *Learn to rejoice in My Kingdom.*

But remember all My children are different. Some are very emotional and excitable. Some are quiet and reserved. All I ask is that each one has their hearts set on Me. That they live by faith in Jesus My Son, and in openness to My Spirit. Remember I am in all things and through all things, big or small. So all of your life, from your eternal destiny to the everyday issues are of interest to Me. When you live in this way you are truly living as a child in My Kingdom.

The areas of brokenness and failure in your life, that you are so conscious of, are also my concern. Though I do not chastise or deal with them harshly. Rather My healing fountain is there to heal, to forgive and to restore. My aim for you, as for all My children, is to move forwards into wholeness. So do trust Me; For as a perfect parent I do know what's best. Freely I gave to the world in Jesus My Son, and freely may you receive through Him.

With deep affection,

Father

I Am With You Always

Psalm 143:6; Matthew 28:20

My child,

Remember I am with you always. I see how you have a thirst deep within you. I see your desire to serve Me. I see also how you struggle with your feelings. You are really too hard on yourself at times. My desire is to fill you with My Spirit. My desire is that you will continually hear My voice.

What do you think I would say to you in these intimate moments? As a good parent, I would say how much I love you. I would hold you in My arms. I would hug you and hold you close to My chest. I would remind you of so many of My promises. And remember they are all yes, and yes again in Jesus. Just relax and trust Me. I see how you struggle with your imagination, but give it to Me. I see how you are tempted. But place these temptations in My hands. Know that I am pleased with you, in all your rest, work and play.

Your ever present,

Father

My Banqueting Table

Jeremiah 15:16 (Living Bible)

My child,

You so often sing, 'He brought Me to His Banqueting Table'. But do you really think about what is on that table? Let Me tell you what is on that table. My Words are on that table. If you will only take them and eat them, you will find they are sweeter than honey. For My words drip with life, My life. These words, are 'Words of Life and Peace'. Take and eat them. Feed upon them. Let them speak to the deep recesses of your heart, so that the soothing balm of these words will heal any of the hurt places that remain.

My banqueting table is a veritable feast of good things. My words come in so many different shapes and sizes. Words for all situations and occasions. The sad thing is that all too often My children sing of the banqueting table and indeed stand right before it. But that is all they do! They don't sit down and feast at My table. Why, O why do they think I provide so much rich fare, on that banqueting table? Is it not because, My banner is a banner of love, and it is waving over them in the gentle breeze of My Spirit.

So learn to stay at the table and feast your heart upon My words. Don't rush on till you have had your fill. Then you will be ready to go out into the world, with the message of Jesus. Having fed upon My words of life at the table, you too will be able to speak some words of life, to a people who are dying and starving, because they don't have any words of life in them. So My invitation to you and all My children as I bring you to My banqueting table is, 'don't just look, tuck in and feast upon it'!

Invitingly,

Father

Walking with Jesus

Nehemiah 8:10(KJV); Psalm 31:5

My younger brother,

I walk beside you every step of the way. For I am truly your older brother. I hold your hand and can guide you over and around all the obstacles you may meet. All you need to do is to keep hold of My hand by faith. All too often my brothers and sisters let go of My hand. I am still beside them every step of the way, but they have lost touch with Me. They have lost that intimate contact I want them to have.

I rejoice and chuckle that you have grasped My hand by faith. How it also tickles My heart that you are rejecting the negative lies that were in your life. It is great that in their place you are embracing the truth about yourself in Me. You can truly be you, as you live in Me. Let's walk together down the path way of life. It may not always be smooth or plain sailing. But let Me share it with you intimately as your brother and as your best friend.

I see you reaching out to hear My words and to see pictures or visions that I plant in your heart. But just relax about these things. I can use you right now, as you are. Do use your understanding of the patterns of brokenness in people's lives to guide you in praying for healing and wholeness, in their lives.

Do learn to laugh with Me, with the pleasure and joy of My kingdom. Why do so many of my children make it a heavy and dull thing! The joy of the Lord is indeed your strength. So hand in hand let us walk together you and Me as brothers.

For I remain forever more your big brother,

Jesus

Getting on with Things

Psalm 1:6

My child,

I do hear your cry to know My guidance and confirmation on what you are doing. But what exactly do you want? Remember My children walk by faith not sight! There are times when you have to get on with those things that are before you and just trust I am in them.

Will you sometimes get things wrong? Yes! But when My children's hearts are set on Me, I do not mind the occasional mistake or wrong turn in the journey. For in the long term or at the end of the ages, I will have accomplished My purposes. The odd twist or turn can be woven into My overall tapestry. The small apparent mistake is incorporated into the master piece of My complete plan for creation, for all people and for you, in this age and the age to come. So do relax!

But often as My children walk by faith in their journey, there do come points where they know they are on the right path. You, as with all My children, do receive confirmation from Me from time to time. So don't think so much about your long-term goals. Pursue your short term ideas and plans. Offer them up to Me. Trust Me. Don't worry about what other people think. For you know I am pleased with you. I am always for you. I am in you and through you, in all you do. So laugh at things with a heavenly chuckle as I do.

Yours chuckling over you,

Father

The Father's Hands

Psalm 31:5; James 1:6

My child,

I love you My child despite your faults and failings. No matter what you think or do, I still go on loving you. For that is the nature of My unconditional love, flowing from the death of My Son on the cross. All people need to do is to connect into this through faith. You are one of those who have found this love and life, through your faith in Jesus. Don't keep asking, 'is my faith sufficient'. It is not the strength of the faith but its direction that matters.

When a child places his small weak hand in the hand of his big strong father it is the father's strength that supports the child. All the child needs to do is to place his hand in that of his father.

Do not keep looking at your feelings; just keep trusting that you are in Me, and I am in you, eternally. Neither should you despise your questioning mind. It was I who gave people the intelligence to ask questions and examine things. However, all such questioning must be carried out from within the 'boat of faith'. Step outside the boat and questioning is like being cast upon the stormy waters without any means of support.

Remember I do love you child; I do accept you. Try to work always from this premise. Then you will begin to experience more freedom and joy.

As ever yours,

Father

The Blanket of God's Love

Deuteronomy 33:12(KJV); Malachi 1:2; 1 John 4:18(KJV)

My little children,

Let My love wrap itself round you like a soft warm fluffy blanket. Snuggle deep down inside it. Feel secure in its protection. Enjoy My presence. My presence of love and security. Unchanging is My Love; unchanging and eternal. Love flowing out from My Son's death at Calvary. Love that glows and grows with the new life of resurrection. Enjoy it my children. Enjoy it, for that is My pleasure.

With deep affection,

Father

God's Constant Heart of Love

Isaiah 49:15; Isaiah 66:13; Luke 15:11-23

My child,

My heart is still towards you and always will be. In human terms a mother or father may grow cold towards their own children. But not so with Me. My love grows stronger. It overcomes anything you can do. Even if you turned your back on Me, I would still go on loving you. (Not that I think you will turn away from Me, for your heart is too set on following Me to do any such thing.)

However, My children who turn away from Me, do not receive My love. It is not that I don't love them, for My love is eternal and unchanging. No, it is that to receive and enjoy My love; My children must have open hearts. They need to turn their faces towards Me and not their backs.

Be assured of My eternal love and continue to open your heart to My love. Let it transform you from within.

With endless love,

Father

Angels Singing

A song of praise to Jesus

Angels singing, heaven ringing
With the Saviours Name.
Earth reflecting, telling of Him
We glimpse His glory now.
Everlasting; king for ever.
Jesus our Lord and King.

On the cross we see him die.
Then lifted up before us high.
The Saviour of the world has come,
Restoring hope to all mankind.

Angels singing ...

One day we will see Him come
And earth restored by the Son of man
The Spirit flowing to this world,
And death is dying now at last.

Angels singing ...

Postscript

At the heart of the really good news of the Christian faith is a relationship. It is not about keeping rules or even primarily having to believe in things. Rather the God who created everything wants a friendship with us. He has made this possible by sending His son Jesus to earth around 2,000 years ago. But that doesn't mean that this truth is either old fashioned or out of date. It is as relevant as it ever was for people of any background or nationality.

When Jesus died and rose again, he opened the door to this relationship with God. The amazing truth is that God wants to be your friend. In fact He wants to be, what He is meant to be, your spiritual parent. (We generally use the word Father to describe this relationship.) But he doesn't desire a distant or cold relationship. He desires to know you closely and intimately. And he wants you to know Him just as intimately.

All we have to do is to allow this. If you like we have to open the door of our inner life, (our heart in Biblical language), to Him. We open this by simple trust that He has invited us into this relationship and this is possible through what Jesus did for all of us in dying on the cross and rising again from the dead. The words we use are not as important as the fact that we have entered into this relationship through Jesus His son. It is this that truly makes us a Christian. That is, we are someone who has put our faith in Jesus. Faith in simple terms is putting our trust in Him. We may vary in the way we express this in our various streams and denominations. But at the heart of all true Christianity is Jesus. So why not open your heart to him today and receive the life He promises you. Hear what he says to you, *'I have come that you may have life, and have it to the full.'*[1]

---

[1] John 10:10 (NIV)

So I encourage you, right now, in your own words to invite Jesus into your life. To trust that through simple act of faith you will have a close and personal relationship with God. If you can't think of your own words to use, then you can use the following prayer:

Father God,

I give my life to you and ask that you will come into my life through Jesus your son. I give you all the things that are wrong and self-centred in my life and trust that you will forgive them because Jesus died on the cross for me. In rising from the dead I now in simple belief trust that you will fill me with life, Your life, through Your Spirit. I offer this prayer in Jesus name,

Amen

Journaling is one way of entering into this intimacy and relationship that God wants you to have. So be bold! Take some paper and a pencil and write down the thoughts that come to you, that you feel are from God. When you have written them, and only when you have written them down, check what they say. See if it matches with character and nature of our loving heavenly Father. Some of the books in the Bibliography may assist you in building up your ease of journaling. I trust His blessing will rest upon you as you walk with Him.

Bibliography

'From the Father's Heart' by Charles Slagle
Destiny Image Publishers USA, 1989 - ISBN: 0-914903-82-9

'An Invitation to Friendship' by Charles Slagle
Destiny Image Publishers USA, 2000 - ISBN: 0-7684-2013-X

'Praise to Soar' by Charles Slagle
Destiny Image Publishers USA, 1994 - ISBN: 1-56043-101-6

'Abba Calling' by Charles Slagle
Destiny Image Publishers USA, 2012 – ISBN: 978-0768441376

'Counselled by God' by Mark Virkler and Patti Virkler
Essence Publishing, 2003 – ISBN: 978-1553065425

'Spirit Born Creativity' by Mark and Patti Virkler
Destiny Image Publishers USA, 1989 – ISBN: 1-56043-004-4

'How to Hear God's Voice' by Mark and Patti Virkler
Destiny Image Publishers USA, 2005 – ISBN: 978-076842318-1

'4 Keys to Hearing God's Voice' by Mark & Patti Virkler
Destiny Image Publishers USA, 2010 – 978-076843248-0

'Surprised by the Voice of God' by Jack Deere
Kingsway Publications, 1996 – ISBN: 0-85476-649-9

Indexes

Letters

Indexes

Indexes

Indexes

Photographs

Photographs taken by the author and copyright to the author:
35; 40; 41; 46; 47; 48; 57; 72; 104.

All other photographs are royalty free from: Dreamstime. www.dreamstime.com
Copyright © 2000-2012 Dreamstime.

Silent Prayer

Sometimes rather than talking to God it is wonderful to just sit in silence and enjoy His presence. This was written as a song to encourage all of us to occasionally use silence as a form of prayer.

In your presence I lay down
In silence you and I are one
Your love is like a candle flame
Silently it sings your refrain

Heaven's song is all around
Gently falls it to the ground
Jesus name is truly peace
A love for all that will not cease

In the stillness you are there
Even quietness is a form of prayer
You are just a breath away
There is nothing that I need to say

Heaven's song ...

Words sometimes get in the way
I really don't know what to say
But I remember you in me
And love is here and sets me free

Heaven's song ...

Lightning Source UK Ltd.
Milton Keynes UK
UKOW03f0118280814

237658UK00001B/42/P